Creating a
Love and Logic
School Culture

Creating a
Love and Logic
School Culture

Jim Fay

Love and Logic

Love and Logic Institute, Inc.
2207 Jackson St
Golden, CO 80401
www.loveandlogic.com
800-338-4065

Love and Logic, Love & Logic, Becoming a Love and Logic Parent, America's Parenting Experts, Love and Logic Magic, 9 Essential Skills for the Love and Logic Classroom, Parenting with Love and Logic, Love and Logic Early Childhood Parenting Made Fun!, Early Childhood Parenting Made Fun! and 🔒 are registered trademarks or trademarks of the Institute For Professional Development, Ltd. and may not be used without written permission expressly granted from the Institute For Professional Development, Ltd.

ISBN# 978-1-935326-09-0

Library of Congress Cataloging-in-Publication Data

Fay, Jim.
  Creating a love and logic school culture / Jim Fay.
     p. cm.
  Includes index.
  ISBN 978-1-935326-09-0
1. School discipline. 2. Motivation in education. 3. School improvement programs. I. Title.
  LB3012.F39 2011
  371.5--dc23
                          2011024593

Cover & Book Design: Michael Snell, Shade of the Cottonwood, L.L.C., Lawrence, KS
Project Coordinator: Kelly Borden

 Published and printed in the United States of America

Contents

A book for school leaders who want to create an environment that promotes student responsibility, staff accountability, and positive school culture. This is not a program, but rather a road map with tools, strategies, and support.

GLENN SPINNIE, PRINCIPAL, JEFFERSON LINCOLN ELEMENTARY

A school's culture has incredible impact on life and learning in the school, yet often goes ignored within school improvement efforts. The school's culture affects student learning in the classroom, behavior in the hallway, and learning and respectful relationships among staff. The ideas, skills, and tools in *Creating a Love and Logic School Culture*, can you improve academic outcomes while building a culture in which students want to learn and great educators want to teach.

DR. BOB SORNSON

The always entertaining Mr. Jim Fay has conveniently collected the very best of the wisdom he has to share with school administrators in this powerful new book. What I have learned from the brilliant and inspiring consultants at Love and Logic saves my life nearly every single day; you will find this book filled to the brim with just such life-saving, practical, and effective techniques and ideas. Every administrator can find something to make their job easier, and their school better for their students, in *Creating a Love and Logic School Culture*.

JENNIFER E. GUTHALS, ED.D., PRINCIPAL, FALL RIVER ELEMENTARY

This is an essential resource for Principals who want to create a school where students have the opportunity to become responsible, caring people by owning their behavior and solving any problems that might accompany that behavior! Whether you have been on the Love and Logic journey for awhile, or are just getting started, this book will provide useful ideas and practical solutions. You will find that you can start using the information immediately!

KATHY ENGELL, PRINCIPAL, KENT PRAIRIE ELEMENTARY

Preface

What Is a Love and Logic School?

If you were to ask me to point out a school where all the staff members use Love and Logic techniques, I'd have to say that I couldn't do that. The authors of the Love and Logic approach have never suggested that our ideas should be mandated as a school-wide discipline plan. However, I can point out many schools in which the Love and Logic approach permeates the very fabric of the school and its community. This culture is achieved when a school staff agrees to a common set of principles about teacher-student interaction. These principles become the beacon, or guiding light, for dealing with students, staff, and parents. The result of this is a positive school culture where teachers love to teach and kids love to learn. The process of creating this culture is the purpose of this book.

If it's so good, why not mandate its use?

I'm sure you've seen what happens when a new program is mandated at your school. There are a few teachers who, for a variety of reasons, feel duty bound to sabotage any mandate. They form small search and destroy teams, going underground with cloak and dagger tactics to undermine the threat of changing any of their comfortable habits. Once a program is mandated, the administrators find themselves in a tug of war, forced to spend unproductive time and energy in an attempt to counter the negative impact these staff members have on morale. To say it bluntly, these teachers seem to have a mission to search and destroy any new program.

For this reason, the authors of the Love and Logic approach strongly suggest that the Love and Logic techniques be offered as a menu of strategies to assist the educational staff in creating a school culture led by the Four Basic Principles of the Love and Logic approach.

LOVE AND LOGIC PRINCIPLE #1:

Whenever possible, maintain the dignity of both the adult and student.
Love and Logic teachers subscribe to the rule, "Treat me with the same respect as I treat you." In other words, Love and Logic educators believe that it's their job to provide the model for mutual respect and dignity.

LOVE AND LOGIC PRINCIPLE #2:

Whenever possible, share the control.
Since the Love and Logic approach is not a permissive approach to working with children, Love and Logic teachers offer healthy control. Kids are allowed to make choices frequently, when their choices don't negatively affect the welfare of others. Teachers make the choices when the good of the class or the school are in question.

LOVE AND LOGIC PRINCIPLE #3:

Whenever possible, share the thinking.
Love and Logic teachers subscribe to the idea that the student should do most of the thinking whenever possible. These teachers understand that questions are more powerful than statements. Whenever possible they turn statements into questions such as, "Wow, throwing food in the cafeteria. Where are you going to eat now that you've lost your cafeteria privileges?"

LOVE AND LOGIC PRINCIPLE #4:

Use the empathy/consequence formula.
Love and Logic teachers understand that leading a statement with empathy raises the odds that students will not *see adults as the source of their own problems. "Oh, no. This is sad. You had alcohol in your locker. Well, no matter how much*

I care for you, I can't protect you from the rules and consequences of the school district. But the good news is that we have eleventh grade here every year, and you can try it again next fall."

What are the characteristics of a love and logic school?

There are many schools that refer to themselves as Love and Logic schools. These are places in which a large percentage of teachers have adopted a number of the *9 Essential Skills for the Love and Logic Classroom*®. Creating this school culture is what this book is all about.

Having worked with and observed schools over the years, I have come to realize that these school staffs subscribe to set of beliefs that serve as a guiding light for teacher-student interaction. As you read this partial list, you will start to view the kind of school culture they create. Please understand that this list is neither complete, nor is it in priority order.

Typical beliefs of love and logic teachers:

1. Classrooms should not be held hostage to the negative behaviors of students.
2. Kids who love their teachers cause fewer classroom disruptions than those who don't.
3. Relationships form the foundation of teaching. Kids work harder and behave better for teachers they like.
4. *Kids want to learn* but often are hampered by their own fears or emotional baggage.
5. The happiest kids are those who have limits and boundaries.
6. The teacher sets the model for respect and dignity.
7. When a student creates a problem, the problem should be handed back to the child in a loving way.
8. Misbehavior and bad decisions are viewed as opportunities for learning as opposed to personal attacks upon the teacher.
9. Kids should solve the problems they create without making problems for anyone else on the face of the earth.
10. Kids are usually capable of solving many problems, especially when offered a menu of options as opposed to dictates or orders.

11. Kids who feel embarrassed in front of their friends will find some form of revenge, even if this revenge is self-destructive.

12. Consequences for misbehavior are most effective when individualized for the student and the situation.

13. Consequences for misbehavior are more effective when stated at a time when both the adult and the student are calm, and when both have had time to think it over.

Who Is the Leader?

I was young, naïve, and totally confused about the true meaning of leadership. As the assistant principal, I sat in my office waiting for several teachers to meet with me for the first time. I was lost in thought about my new goals for the school and the grand impact I could make, being in charge of discipline.

As they walked into the room, the questions were already flying.

"What are you going to do about discipline?"

"I'm here to support you. I understand that's the reason I was assigned here," I squeaked.

"We want to know what you're going to do with the kids who get sent to the office. The last assistant principal didn't do anything. Kids liked coming to the office. She just talked to them and let them run errands. We don't send them down here to have a good time. There has to be some consistency. We can't teach if there isn't a little discipline around here.

"So here's our solution. We developed a matrix so that every kid would get treated exactly the same. It's all in the student handbook, in case you haven't read that yet."

"Well," I said, "I've read the handbook and I can tell you that I'm a law and order guy. You send the kids to me and you'll get the support you need."

Sudden Role Reversal

At that point, the teachers all became my supervisors. In fact, I now had 50 different supervisors who were never happy with the way I handled discipline referrals. Each teacher had a different expectation about how I was to deal with the discipline problems that ended up in my office. The more they complained about my work, the harder I worked to make them happy, but to no avail. I can't count the number of times a teacher would roar into my office with, "What did you do with my student? I didn't send him down here to have a good time."

Typical Student/Principal Scenario

The following scenario played itself out over and over for the next few years:

"Why are you here?"
"I don't know. Teacher sent me."
"Why did she send you?"
"I don't know. Ask her. I didn't do 'nothin.' "
"I don't buy that. Now what were you doing."
"I don't know. The other kids were messing around, and she told me to go to the office. She's always on my case."
"Come on. She didn't send you for nothing. Now what was it?"
"I guess maybe I was talking a little."
"Fine. Did she tell you to stop?"
"No. She just said for me to go to see you."
"Let's see if I've got it. You were just talking a little. Without asking you to stop, she just sent you to the office. Now why would she do that?"
"Ask her. Maybe she hates me. She doesn't do anything to her favorites."

I didn't think that was true, so I told him that the next time he was sent to the office it would result in a parent conference, and I sent him back to class.

Now it was time for the teacher to tell about his return to the classroom. See if this sounds familiar.

"Well, I can tell you," replied the teacher, "he came back to class looking like the cat that ate the canary, all smug and grinning at his friends."

"So I asked him, 'What did Mr. Fay do?' "

"Nothing."

"What do you mean nothing?"

"We just talked."

"Let me tell you, Mr. Fay, I'm livid! I didn't send him down there to just talk and have a good time! How am I supposed to teach if you don't do anything about these out of control kids? No wonder we don't have any discipline around here."

"Wait a minute," I would respond. "Aren't the kids better after I send them back to the classroom?"

"That's not the point. When I send kids to the office for discipline, I don't want them coming back to the classroom acting like they had a good time!"

Through the grapevine, during my early days as a principal, I frequently heard teachers saying, "We don't get any administrative support." And since I had subconsciously accepted that the teachers were my immediate supervisors, I just worked harder to please them.

Without knowing it, I was in a vicious cycle. The more I accepted the responsibility of solving their problems, the less responsible teachers felt for learning to work effectively with kids. Soon I had kids lined up in my office for all kinds of little problems that should have been solved in the classroom.

The less responsibility the teachers took in dealing with discipline, the more time they had to criticize my work. And the less time I had to support the staff in the right way.

It never occurred to me that each of the staff members had a different vision of what support looked like, until one day I woke up to the fact that not all the teachers complained about my lack of support.

Starting to See the Light

One bright day it occurred to me that the teachers who never complained about lack of support were the ones who talked to me and gave me a good description of their view of support. Now that I was starting to understand this, it was easy for me recognize that I wasn't really supporting the staff, in spite of the fact that I didn't have a written plan that said, "My daily goal each day is to find a way to leave teachers feeling unsupported and unappreciated."

"So," I had to say to myself, "they're right. I may not be providing support. I probably view support one way. Each teacher may be viewing it a different way. So I provide support by acting out of my own view, while at the same time it might be opposite of the view of the teacher."

As this phenomenon occurred to me, I could see that I needed a way to discover each teacher's view of support without having to be a mind reader or amateur psychologist, and without making my job harder. This is one of the many techniques you will read about in this book.

CHAPTER 2

More of the Same

The teachers at our school voiced their solutions both loudly and clearly. They were:

1. We need better rules.
2. We need the kids to follow the rules.
3. We need all the teachers to enforce the rules.
4. We need the principal to enforce the rules.
5. We need consistency. Everyone should enforce the rules as prescribed in the student handbook.

Educators had used this approach for years, so they did too. They chose a "Discipline Committee." The committee met and established rules. They then developed a matrix, describing the consequences that would be meted out for each rule infraction. This matrix also outlined consequences that increased in severity with each subsequent infraction.

It looked like this:

First offense: Warning
Second offense: Loss of privilege
Third offense: Parent contact

Third offense: Parent conference
Fourth offense: In-school suspension
Fifth offense: Out of school suspension

The idea was that kids would know in advance how their misbehavior would affect them at each level of infraction. Not only did they know what would happen to them, they knew that every child would be treated exactly the same.

The reasoning behind this was that parents could not complain if the kids knew in advance about the rules and consequences, and that fair treatment was extended to all the kids without exception.

This appears to make sense, until it's put into action. What happened at this school was no different from the experiences of hundreds, if not thousands, of other schools. Finding two teachers who view the world exactly the same is difficult, if not impossible. Finding two teachers who view the behavior of a child and agree upon the severity of the infraction is close to impossible.

Problem number one: Do we all see things the same way?

All humans view the world through their own very special filters that are developed over a lifetime of experiences. Not only are our experiences all a little different, our perceptions of those experiences are different.

For instance, two teachers seeing a student running in the hall could see the rules infraction in two different ways. Teacher Number One says to herself, "Kids sure like to run. I wish I could do that," while teacher Number Two thinks, "This is a major crime scene."

Teacher Number One does not believe in the running rule and ignores the problem. Teacher Number Two sees running and thinks, "See, that's the problem with this school. The other teachers are not being consistent. No wonder we have discipline problems. This school is out of control."

The same thing happens in the office. I remember little Philip, a first grader who "mooned" his classmates on the playground. He thought it was pretty cool until ending up in the office for discipline.

After sitting on the bench waiting for me to see him, and after thinking about it some more, he appeared to be pretty embarrassed, if not humiliated, by his own actions. The more I talked with him, the more I sensed his embarrassment. I thought that the most effective punishment would be for him to have to return to class and face the teacher and his friends.

Sensing this, I said, "Maybe it would be best if you just go back to class and think about the possibility of apologizing to your teacher and the class." Tears filled his eyes, and I could see that doing that was about the last thing he wanted to do. I got the idea that he might rather have his fingernails pulled out with pliers.

But here I was, between a rock and a hard place. Our discipline matrix said that this kind of rules violation required a three-day suspension, not a return to class.

I thought to myself. "If he goes home, he's off the hook except for the angry lecture he'll get from his parents. Three days will be enough for him to forget about it, and three days is enough time for the class to forget about it.

"But if I do what I think fits this situation best, the teachers are going to say that I'm not following the matrix, and that they are not getting the support they deserve. If I follow the matrix, Philip gets an easy pass on his bad behavior."

Our nation has seen many such situations where kids violate the rules slightly off center and administrators, caught in the crossfire, follow the matrix only to be the laughing stock of talk shows, or finding themselves on the front page of both local and national newspapers.

An example that comes to mind has to do with the elementary school student who made a replica of a gun out of LEGOs, brought it to school for show and tell, and found himself being expelled for having a gun at school.

My guess is that the school administrators said to themselves, "If we follow this Zero Tolerance Policy, we will be the laughing stock of the nation. If we don't, we will look like we are soft on school security, and unsupportive of the district rules regarding school safety. We lose no matter which way we go."

Even though I didn't have to suffer the indignities of the school officials who did this, I have had many times when I felt that my hands were tied by a school discipline plan that prescribed consequences in advance instead of treating each child and each situation on a case-by-case basis.

Problem number two:
This approach sews the seeds of morale problems.

Let's revisit Teacher Number One and Teacher Number Two and their view of Winston's running in the hall.

Teacher Number One has friends on the staff with similar opinions. Teacher Number One finds others with whom she can commiserate with. During their breaks, they often find themselves talking about how they would like to see the school run. "If some of the other teachers would just lighten up a little and enjoy the kids, this place would run a little better."

Teacher Number Two's friends do the same thing except their solutions are different. "If the other teachers would just enforce the rules the way they're supposed to, this school would run a lot better and the kids would behave so we could teach for a change. And if the principal would show a little leadership he/she'd make those teachers follow the discipline plan."

Little by little, staff morale deteriorates as teachers use the actions and the beliefs of others as the reason for any lack of effectiveness.

This "Systems-Based or Cook Book Approach to Discipline" tends to pit staff member against staff member. How sad! The original purpose of this approach was to develop consistency instead of pitting professional against professional.

Problem number three:
The need to develop new skills is reduced.

As long as teachers can use the actions of others as the reason for lack of effectiveness, there is little need or motivation for them to develop better ways of working with children.

And the Discord Continues

The school year was over. The kids were scattered to the winds, and the teachers were off for the summer. I sat in my office and thought, "I feel just like the little exhausted gerbil falling off of the treadmill."

How did this happen? Another year was off the books and I didn't get to cross off very many of the items on my goals list. How would I explain this to the superintendent? Where did all my time go? I came in early each day. I stayed late each evening. And, oh, yeah, there weren't many days when I sat down for a leisurely lunch, instead of eating on the go. I needed to calm down and figure out where my time went.

I put my feet up, closed my eyes and the answer soon came my way. I'd spent much of my time doing what my teachers told me to do on their office referrals:

- "I'm sending Mike to you because he never comes to class with a pencil. Do something."
- "Jennifer keeps talking in class. Do something."
- "Alisha and Megan are being inappropriate in class. Do something."
- "Jose was tardy. Do something."
- "Andrew talked back to me. Do something."

- "Tracy won't do her work. Do something."
- "I'm not having Carmillo back in class until he apologizes. Do something."

Out of curiosity, I looked into my office referral file and found that I had been dealing with a spectacular number of situations like this each day. No wonder I didn't have time to be a leader. The teachers had me on a short leash, dealing with all kinds of situations that they could, and should, have handled themselves.

I Had Become the Servant—Of the Teachers

Another realization hit me between the eyes. Not only had I spent lots of time being supervised by my staff, I'd spent considerable time defending the way I'd handled the kids who were sent to the office for discipline.

"This is disappointing," I thought. "Not only did I dedicate my time trying to make things better for the teachers, they didn't even appreciate my efforts." A number of the teachers had been quick to criticize my work:

- "What did you do with Alisha and Megan? They are still acting out!"
- "What did you do with Carmillo? I didn't send him to the office to have a good time!"
- "If you were a little tougher on these kids, I could get some teaching done."

I'd even gotten complaints when I'd done a good job. "What did you do with Richie? I didn't send him to the office to have a good time."

"Wait a minute. Wasn't he any better when he returned to class?"

"Well, yes he was, but he waltzed back into class like he'd just returned from Disney World. I don't need that kind of attitude."

I'd swear that there were a few, not all, but a few of the teachers who wouldn't have been happy unless they saw drops of blood from the office back to the classroom.

Then I thought to myself for the first time, "I really can't make these teachers do things they don't want to do. I don't see why they have any more power over me than I have over them. Maybe they shouldn't be my supervisors after all."

A Solution

I met with the staff the next fall with a new plan.

"I've had some time to think about discipline because it's important to me that I support you in that area and I've come up with a plan.

"I've been accepting office referrals, trying to do my best to help, and it appears that it's not been as effective as you'd like.

"Here's how things will be handled this year. I will continue to accept office referrals for discipline in two ways and you are free to decide which way you want to do it.

"You may send a student to me when he/she is making it difficult for you to teach, or when he/she is making it difficult for the other kids to learn. The purpose of this is to allow the kid to think it over and cool down.

"Please know that I will not deal with the student other than to find him/her a place to sit. If that student comes back to class and says that I didn't do anything, he/she is telling the truth.

"If you actually want me to deal with the situation, tell the student that we will do something about his/her behavior. Then make an appointment for the two of us to talk with him/her. I will no longer be dealing with these office referrals alone. If you want me to counsel with a student, you'll need to be present.

"In other words, we are going to work on discipline with kids together. This way they will hear the consequences from you instead of me, because I want students to learn that the teacher is the ultimate authority figure here, not the principal.

"Now, if you have a particular disciplinary action you'd like applied, talk with me in advance so I can tell you whether or not I have the support of the superintendent to do that."

The Staff's Reaction

One teacher was quick to complain. "Wait a minute. It's your job is to make these kids behave so we can teach."

I wanted to defend this with references to research in this area, but thought better of debating the issue.

"That may or may not be true, but many of you didn't like the way I did it in the first place."

Another teacher voiced concern. "I suppose now if one of my students has a problem in the lunchroom, I have to take my time and make an appointment with you."

"No, the lunchroom supervisors can handle that. You only need to make an appointment when you want to have an appointment. You deal with the problems that are under your direct supervision and others will do the same."

Another voice was raised. "What if there is a fight or some other kind of safety violation. What then?"

"Send the kids to me for a cool down. Then I'll visit with you and we can decide what's best. We'll try to support each other the best way we can, given the situation. I'm sure we can work it out by talking to each other. If all else fails, we might try to apply common sense even though I'm not sure common sense is on the latest State Department of Education List of Approved Programs."

I was hoping that this feeble attempt at humor would ease the tension. Some of the teachers giggled while some of them frowned. I should just have kept my mouth under control, but it was just too tempting and felt too good at the time. Have you ever have a time like that?

"But what if it's some kind of dangerous situation," asked another teacher.

"Remove the child immediately. We'll work from there. The important thing to remember is that consequences for misbehavior don't have to be immediate.

"This new procedure is new to all of us. We'll tweak it along the way. The important thing for me is that kids start to see teachers as real authority figures here."

How Did It Work?

As you can guess, teachers were no longer making appointments to deal with little issues such as forgotten class materials or crusty looks from kids. The number of students I was dealing with dwindled.

Kids could no longer work the teacher against the principal and vice versa. I was able to hear both sides of each story and kids started to see teachers and administrators as a team.

I remember visiting with one teacher prior to a discipline appointment. "What do you think we need to do with this kid?" I asked.

"I think that a couple of days of suspension might wake him up."

"Good. Let's do that. I'll ask you in front of him what should be done. You can talk about a suspension. Then I can say something about him being lucky to have a wise teacher. You suspend him for two days and I'll just nod in agreement."

The student was shocked. "Hey, teachers can't suspend kids. Only principals can do that!"

"Well, pal. There's a first time for everything. We'll look forward to seeing you in a couple of days. We talked with your mom this morning. I don't think she will be as surprised as you are. Good luck."

Over a period of time, I came to believe that this approach to dealing with office referrals was long over due. It was one of the best things I had done for that school.

The list of advantages goes on and on:

1. Office referrals are fewer.
2. Discipline conferences are more effective.
3. Communication is increased between principal and teachers.
4. Teachers soon come to realize that they can handle much of the discipline on their own, and don't need the appointment.
5. The principal has an opportunity to model positive interactions with students.
6. Teachers can't go the lounge and complain that nothing happens when they send a kid to the office, since they are part of the session.

7. The teachers and students have a chance to get their emotions under control while waiting for an appointment time.
8. Teachers discover that delayed consequences are more effective than immediate ones.
9. The principal has more time to do what principals are paid to do.
10. Students get to see staff members working in harmony and can no longer drive a wedge between teachers and administrators.

A Principles-Based Approach to Discipline

After several years of experiencing the downside of a cook book/systems-based approach to discipline, it finally dawned on me that we were spending way too much time on discipline.

While claiming that we were consistent in applying discipline, the opposite was true. Instead of motivating teachers to learn more effective techniques of discipline, the system provided opportunities for teachers to blame other staff members for their lack of success. Not only was the system unsuccessful, it contributed to morale problems.

The difficulty of getting teachers to see the damaging effects of yelling, threatening, lecturing, and other punitive measures was a constant problem. Each time I questioned or complained about these teacher behaviors I found myself in a defensive position. I found myself trying to prove that these techniques were not good for kids. I bet you can guess how successful my efforts were.

There were always a few staff members who seemed dedicated to trying to scare the kids into behaving. These teachers had a multitude of excuses for their tactics. They claimed that lack of parent support, lack of administrative support, non-caring kids, state and federal guidelines, etc., left them with no other options than to yell at kids or threaten office referrals, in-school suspension, and/or detention. They were great finger pointers, but seemed to feel little need to develop new skills to manage classrooms and prevent misbehavior.

When the Horse Dies, It's Time to Quit Riding

Does all of this ring a bell? Do you believe that schools have experimented with cook book/systems-based discipline plans long enough without great improvement? If so, I'm here to suggest a different path to effective school discipline where we spend less time dealing with disruptive behaviors and more time enjoying the art of teaching. It's called the Principles-Based Approach.

A Principles-Based Discipline Plan recognizes the difficulty of getting all staff members to react to situations in a consistent way. However, the possibility of getting people to react consistently to a set of basic principles is much easier to achieve.

Consistency Takes On Another Form

For instance, getting all teachers to enforce a rule in the same way is nearly impossible. Getting teachers to deal with a situation consistently with a basic principle is different.

Suppose that everyone on the staff has agreed that attempting to maintain both the dignity of the child and the adult would serve as a guiding principle. There are as many different ways of dealing with a rule violation in a dignified way as there are creative people.

Let's use Winston's violation of the No Running in the Hall rule. Mr. Jackson deals with it by saying to Winston, "Pal, I worry about someone getting hurt. Stand by me until the hall is cleared and then show me that you can do it right. Thank you." Winston's reason for running backfires on him. Mr. Jackson hands the problem back to Winston.

Mrs. Jamison reacts in a different way, still maintaining her dignity and that of Winston. "Winston, I know you can do better than that. How about going back to the room and showing me that you can do it right?

Thank you." Winston's reason for running backfires on him in a different way. However, the problem he created has still become his own problem.

Ms. Waller sees this as a more serious case and says, "Winston, I've seen this too many times. I need an appointment to visit with you about it. Would you rather meet with me at 3:00 or 3:20? Do you need to call your mom and let her know that you are going to be late? Thank you." Winston faces a different kind of consequence.

Each teacher enforced the rule in his/her own special way. They were consistent with the school policy that required teachers to enforce rules. All three of these teachers were consistent with the basic principle regarding dignity while being totally inconsistent with each other. With this approach, each teacher can view and deal with the problem in his/her own way, thus deserving the support of the administrator because he/she enforced the no running rule.

**Teachers Are More Inclined To Enforce Rules
When Not Limited in Their Methods**

The Principles-Based Approach

Schools and classrooms need to be Law and Order Places so rules for student behavior are created. They are usually titled, *Expectations and Rules for the Orderly Operation of Our School*. Staff members are expected to enforce those rules.

In the beginning, a set of Core Beliefs are developed. Chapter Five describes the process for their development and acceptance by teachers and administrators. These Core Beliefs serve as a code of ethics or guiding light for the way professionals in this school will deal with discipline problems.

Once the Core Beliefs are developed and published, they are posted throughout the school. They are also included in student handbooks. Teachers are then encouraged to handle violations of rules on a case-by-case basis, based on how they view the violation and the behavior history of the student. Administrative support is assured provided the actions of the teacher do not violate the school's Core Beliefs.

In the example of Winston and his running in the halls, each of the teachers would have the support of the principal because their actions didn't violate the school's Core Beliefs.

Let's suppose one of the teachers had handled it in another way, yelling, "Winston, I'm sick and tired of seeing you running in the hall! You know the rules! Now you get yourself back to your room and do it again. Am I going to have to give you an office referral?"

Having violated the Core Belief about maintaining dignity of the adult and child, the principal's support is not available. And in a Love and Logic school the principal would require the teacher to explain why his/her actions are in accordance with the Core Beliefs.

Chapter Eleven will describe a simple method for the principal to confront teachers who do not live with or act in accordance with the code of ethics established through the process of developing the school's Core Beliefs.

Advantages of a Principles-Based Approach

1. Teachers are free to deal with student misbehavior based on unique circumstances and unique views of the rule violation.
2. Teachers cannot blame other staff members for their lack of success in dealing with discipline.
3. The principal has an easy "yardstick" to evaluate the performance of teachers relative to the ways they handle discipline.
4. Teachers are more motivated to learn and/or develop more creative and effective ways of dealing with students.
5. Parents have a better way of understanding how teachers work with their kids.
6. Parents are more supportive when they believe that each child is treated as a unique individual and each situation is treated as a unique situation.
7. Staff morale is higher as teachers feel that they are being treated as professionals.
8. The Core Belief document can serve to improve parent/teacher conferences when there are questions about the actions of the staff. (Chapter Fourteen)
9. The Core Belief can be a great tool in staff hiring. (Chapter Fourteen)

TWO APPROACHES TO SCHOOL-WIDE DISCIPLINE

Cook Book/System-Based Program

Rules are developed.

Expectations are established that students will follow the rules.

Staff members meet to determine a set of punishments or consequences for violations. These are established in advance in a sequential manner. Everyone knows what is going to happen the first time there is an infraction, the second time, the third time, etc.

Expectations are placed upon all staff members to impose punishments in a manner consistent with the school-wide discipline plan.

Typical Results

Staff members who have difficulty dealing with students often blame it on the fact that others are not enforcing the rules consistently. "I wouldn't be having this trouble if the others would just enforce the rules the way they should!"

Staff members often complain that others allow the students to get away with infractions. The staff frequently becomes fragmented. Staff morale is usually low.

Others often complain that the punishments just don't quite fit the crimes.

Many staff members ignore infractions because they do not agree with the prescribed set of punishments or consequences.

Students often use this to their advantage and manipulate the adults.

The staff cries for more rules and more consistency.

Numerous complaints are often expressed about teachers and children.

Principles-Based Program

Rules are developed and posted.

Expectations are established that students will follow the rules.

Staff members are expected to enforce the rules and take action when rules are violated.

Staff members meet to agree upon a common set of principles, which, in turn, are the basis for all decisions regarding the treatment of discipline problems.

Consistency is achieved when discipline situations are handled in a manner consistent with an agreed set of principles. Recognizing that it is almost impossible to achieve total consistency of beliefs and reactions within a staff, teachers are encouraged to discipline students by selecting from a range of consequences with the understanding that the consequence or counseling used is consistent with the set of values or principles commonly agreed upon by the staff as a whole.

Typical Results

Staff members are neither allowed nor encouraged to blame their problems on the techniques used by others. It is understood that each person will develop special relationships with children and that these will be different in every case.

This leaves staff members with the responsibility of learning how to respond to students and set limits in effective ways rather than expecting others to do it for them.

Staff members find a need to develop a range of consequences that can be used in different situations according to the severity of the infraction.

Teachers feel like professionals.

Developing the
School Core Beliefs

Step One:

You may copy the form, Creating Your Core Beliefs, found on page 25 or call the Love and Logic Institute and have a black and white master sent to you. Reproduce a copy for every teacher.

Step Two:

Provide a copy for every teacher with the following instructions: "Go through these different beliefs and circle five to six of the ones that best represent your beliefs about working with kids. Your goal is to pick the ones that you'd be proud to associate with your name. Pretend that there is going to be an article in the local newspaper about you and your philosophy of dealing with kids. The article will include your beliefs about dealing with children. You will have a few days to study the list and make your decisions."

The "Creating Your Core Beliefs" list was purposely written to create some discussion and/or concerns about the wording. Instruct the teachers to stick with the wording. With some faculties, we find that they want to start changing the wording to the point that the beliefs become "weasel words," instead of a true commitment or code of ethics. Take this opportunity to listen to and empathize with their concerns but try to stick with the wording. After the Core Beliefs document is in use for a period of time, it can be reviewed and modified as necessary.

Step Three:

Call a faculty meeting, asking teachers to bring their list with them. Create some random groups of four to six teachers. Ask each group to pool their thoughts and come up with fix to six of the beliefs that they can all agree upon.

Step Four:

Once all the groups have arrived at total agreement on five to six of these beliefs, hold a vote. Have the leader of each group report on the decisions of his/her group. *It is crucial that every teacher is present at this time and can see how each of the groups voted.*

As you call on each group for their answers, ask if all are in agreement. In the event that they are not in total agreement, send them back to work until this happens.

Tally the results in front of the entire staff and create a Core Beliefs document for your school.

Caution!

1. Do not hold this meeting if there is anyone absent. This set of Core Beliefs will become a powerful tool for guiding teachers in their decisions about discipline. It's also a powerful tool for holding teachers accountable for their actions. It will have little value if a teacher can say, "I didn't agree, or I didn't vote on the Core Beliefs document."
2. There will be more about holding teachers accountable for their actions in Chapter Seven. Don't give away your power and responsibility to hold staff members accountable for the way they treat students in your school.
3. *Never tally the results in private.*
4. Don't bother with creating this set of Core Beliefs if you don't intend to enforce compliance. Many schools have mission statements, etc.,

that are no more than a set of "weasel words." Mission statements like these are ignored, and are less than worthless. In fact, these kinds of mission statements are of little value when they have no connection to specific expectations.

5. Remember that there are simple and effective ways to hold teachers accountable to the Core Beliefs document. These skills are easy to learn and easy to use. They will be discussed later in this book.

Occasionally I'm asked about what to do if the staff picks Core Beliefs that are negative or punitive. After doing this exercise with many different schools, we've found that even the most negative or punitive teachers seem to identify the same positive Core Beliefs. Even though their actions are frequently punitive, teachers, in general tend to identify beliefs that are supportive of children. You will find an example of the typical results of this exercise on page 31.

But What If It Does Happen?

In the unlikely event that this does happen, I suggest that the principal ask the staff to present some empirical research that supports their decision. By no means would I take on the burden of proving that their choice was wrong. I'd let them carry the burden of proving to me that they are right. If push comes to shove, I might tell the staff that I, personally, could not be proud to be associated with these beliefs about working with kids and would veto their choice. In other words, "the buck stops here" with real leaders.

Step Five:

Once the Core Beliefs document is developed, tell the staff members that they are each free to enforce the school rules in any way they see fit, provided that their actions do not violate the Core Beliefs. At this time, you can let the staff know that training in classroom management skills that support the intentions of the Core Beliefs will be offered to anyone who is interested.

Even though I believe that the Love and Logic strategies are the most effective ways to handle most situations, I strongly urge that they not be mandated. I'm sure you have had plenty of experience with what happens when teachers are forced to adopt new programs, etc.

Once the Core Beliefs document is developed you have, in effect, created a Code of Ethics for your staff. This Code of Ethics is going to become one of your most valuable tools in several important areas:

1. Supervising and leading the staff toward positive relationships with students
2. Holding staff accountable for positive and effective student/staff interactions
3. Building positive community support
4. Dealing with difficult parent conferences
5. Identifying and hiring skilled staff members

As this book progresses you will see, and come to appreciate, the many benefits of this document.

Now that the staff has created the Core Beliefs document, it is time to move on to developing your school-wide discipline plan.

Creating Your School's Core Beliefs

When working with students in a disciplinary situation choose five to seven of these to create a set of core beliefs for your school. This is your code of ethics or your promise to students and parents about the treatment of disciplinary situations.

1. I believe that every attempt should be made to maintain the dignity of both the adult and the student.

2. I believe that students should know that misbehavior makes adults angry.

3. I believe that students should know that misbehavior results in loss of privileges.

4. I believe that adults should be respected because they are the adults.

5. I believe that students should be guided and expected to solve the problems they create without making problems for anyone else.

6. I believe that students should expect rewards for good behavior.

7. I believe that students should be given the opportunity to make decisions and live with the results, whether the consequences are good or bad.

8. I believe that misbehavior should be handled with natural consequences instead of punishments whenever possible.

9. I believe that students should know that the adults are the bosses and in control at all times.

10. I believe that students should have the opportunity to tell their side of the story (due process hearing) when consequences appear to be unfair.

11. I believe that teachers are responsible for raising student self-esteem.

12. I believe that school problems should be handled by school personnel and that criminal activity should be referred to the proper authorities.

13. I believe that misbehavior should be viewed as an opportunity for individual problem solving and preparation for the real world as opposed to a personal attack on the school or staff.

14. I believe that students should pay for repeat misbehaviors.

15. I believe that it is best if a student does most of the thinking.

16. I believe that there should be a logical connection between misbehavior and resulting consequences.

17. I believe that it is the administrator's job to make students behave so that teachers can teach.

18. I believe that parents should punish their children when they misbehave at school.

19. I believe that prescribed punishments for rules infractions are an important part of maintaining discipline.

20. I believe that every student and every rules infraction should be treated the same way.

The School-Wide Discipline Plan

Rules and expectations for appropriate behavior can be divided into two categories. One set of rules should deal with public safety, much like city, state, and federal laws. These statutes or laws have prescribed fines and/or punishments.

In the school district, these rules are established by the Board of Education. Violations of these rules have prescribed consequences that ideally apply to everyone on an equal basis. As I say this (with tongue in cheek), you need to hold your breath because I believe that they should even apply to the All-State Quarterback, even if that means losing the State Championship this year. Now I know that this is a stretch, but I bet you get my point.

As a school principal, I like this. It gives me a chance to provide consequences without being the bad guy. It gives me a chance to enforce the rules while separating the deed from the doer.

"Wow, pal. This is really unfortunate. You brought alcohol on the school bus. No matter how much I care for you I can't save you from the consequences the Board of Education lays down for this kind of thing. But fortunately, we offer eleventh grade every year at this school and the rules say that you can try it again. Sure hope to see you again next fall."

The second set of rules is established at the building level and supports the orderly operation of daily life at the building level. Given the recognition of individual differences, and given the ideas set forth in chapter four, the enforcement of these rules is determined on a case-by-case basis.

Feel free to use the prototype discipline plan offered here.

PROTOTYPE DISCIPLINE PLAN
Expectations and Rules for Student Conduct
Severence County School District R-1
Wilmot Middle School

Standards of Student Safety and Security

The school board has set forth rules and expectations addressing student safety and security. Much like the rules that govern our cities, violations of these rules carry penalties, fines, and consequences, etc. that are prescribed by law. The purpose of penalties under these federal, state, and local laws is to insure an orderly and safe society.

The Board of Education sets the standards for safety and security and has set penalties for violation of these standards. These standards address the safety and security of both children and school staff. They are not up for interpretation at the local school level, just as the laws for our state, city, and/or county statutes are not up for interpretation or revision by local school administrators.

DISTRICT RULES

The following is a list of rules established by the Board of Education:
The penalties or consequences for violating these rules cannot be excused or changed by local school administrators or staff.

Safety and Security Rules

(Fill in this space with district rules that usually cover, but are not limited to the following:)

- Possession or use of illegal drugs
- Possession or use of alcohol
- Acts or threats of violence
- Possession of weapons
- Possession or use of dangerous articles
- Acts or threats of bullying
- Acts or threats of sexual harassment

Penalties for Violation of District Rules

The following penalties have been established by the Board of Education, Severence County School District R-1.

(Fill this section in with a copy of the District Rules)

Safety and Security Rules

All district rules related to safety and security are in effect at all times at the local school level.

SCHOOL RULES

Rules and Expectations Supporting the Orderly Operation of the School and the Educational Process

Rules and expectations covered in this section are designed to meet the following goals:

1. Maintain an orderly school operation.
2. Maintain optimal learning opportunities for students. School facilities and classrooms must be free of behaviors that interfere with teaching and learning.
3. Help students develop skills and behaviors necessary for healthy social interaction, both present and future.
4. Help students learn how their decisions affect the quality of theirs and others lives.
5. Help students develop responsibility and character.

Wilmot Middle School Rules

1. Treat others with the same respect with which you are treated by the adults in this school.

2. Your actions, dress, possessions, etc., may not cause a problem for anyone else.

   Problem actions include, but are not limited to:
   (Fill in this section as needed.)

   Problems related to dress include, but are not limited to:
   (Fill in this section as needed.)

   Problems related to possessions include, but are not limited to:
   (Fill in this section as needed.)

3. If your actions, dress, or possessions cause a problem for anyone else, you will be asked to solve that problem.

4. If you cannot solve the problem, or choose not to, staff members will impose upon you an appropriate consequence. This consequence will depend upon the situation and the person or persons involved. Staff members will use their best judgment based upon the information they have at the time.

5. If students and/or parents feel that the consequences are unfair, they should request a "due process" hearing.

A due process hearing does not need to be formal in nature. It is simply a time for concerned individuals to meet and share information related to the situation in question. In the event that this discussion provides additional information that sheds different light on the situation, or shows the consequences to be unfair, the consequences may be changed or eliminated to better fit the unique situation.

Core Beliefs that Guide Enforcement of School Rules and Expectations

Each student is a unique individual with unique personal, social, and educational needs.
   As a result, every disciplinary situation is unique in nature. Consequences for misbehavior provide the best learning value when matched to the unique student and the unique situation. The odds for children learning from their mistakes increase dramatically when children see a reasonable connection between their behavior and the resulting consequences.

The Wilmot Middle School staff dedicates itself to following a set of core beliefs that provide a guide for dealing with student discipline. These core beliefs guide our attempts to individualize disciplinary procedures and to help students see reasonable connections between their behavior and the resulting consequences.

Since these core beliefs provide the guiding light for our professional decisions, the staff encourages parents to bring concerns and questions to us in the event that we operate in ways that appear to be inconsistent with these core beliefs.

Wilmot Middle School Staff Core Beliefs

The following list of core beliefs outlines the professional actions and attitudes of all staff members in this school.

1. Every attempt will be made to maintain the dignity and self-respect of both the student and the teacher.
2. Students will be guided and expected to solve their problems, or the ones they create, without creating problems for anyone else.
3. Students will be given opportunities to make decisions and live with the consequences, be they good or bad.
4. Misbehavior will be handled with natural or logical consequences instead of punishment, whenever possible.
5. Misbehavior will be viewed as an opportunity for individual problem solving and preparation for the real world as opposed to a personal attack on school or staff.
6. Students are encouraged to request a "due process hearing" whenever consequences appear to be unfair.
7. School problems will be handled by school personnel. Criminal activity will be referred to the proper authorities.

Individual Classroom Rules

1. Treat your teacher with the same respect with which he/she treats you.
2. Your actions may not cause a problem for anyone else.
3. If you cause a problem, you will be asked to solve it.
4. If you cannot solve the problem, or choose not to, I will do something. What I do will depend upon the situation and the person involved.

If I do something that appears to be unfair, whisper to me, "I'm not sure that's fair," and we will talk about it.

This document is offered to serve as a comprehensive discipline plan for your school. Feel free to copy it and amend it to fit your individual district and school needs.

Individualizing Discipline

The concept of allowing teachers to treat discipline problems on a case-by-case basis can be a paradigm shift for some teachers. Even though the results of following a cook book/systems-based approach is often unsuccessful, this approach can provide comfort for many teachers. It can provide an excuse to blame someone else if things go wrong. Teachers can blame it on lack of administrator support, lack of consistency among teachers, or a flawed system. This is all much more comforting than having to look at one's self, one's own techniques or skills, or the student/teacher relationship.

This came to light years ago when I first consulted with a school in the development of a principles-based approach. I didn't have the benefit of the form, Creating Your School's Core Beliefs. As a result, the process took much more time. The teachers wanted to focus on rules and punishments and had a difficult time looking inward to what they believed.

In spite of this, they finally came up with a set of beliefs similar to the ones listed in Chapter Four. Once this was finished, I said to the teachers, "Okay, now we have a set of rules and we have, in effect, a set of Core Beliefs that will serve as a guiding light for all of you as you deal with discipline. Each of you is free to handle any rule violation on a case-by-case basis. Your principal is going to honor your approach to dealing with the problem as long as your actions do not violate any of these Core Beliefs."

It just happened that the principal of that school is the now famous Dr. Betsy Geddes. Her ears perked up when she heard me make this statement. Immediately she got me off to the side saying, "Jim, how can you say that to my staff? If they all get to decide how they are going to handle discipline, I won't have any control."

Dr. Geddes laughs about that to this day as she often tells her audiences about it. She says, "That was the day the light went on for me when Jim turned to me and replied, 'Betsy, you don't have any control now. What's going to be different?' "

When Dr. Geddes speaks, she goes on to explain that she had little or no control over teachers once they shut their classroom doors. They were basically doing what they wanted to do. However, once the Core Beliefs document was developed she had a tool that gave her much more influence over how students were treated. This will be presented in Chapter Eleven.

It was only a week later that I received a phone call from Betsy. "Jim, you've got to help the teachers. For years they've been locked into a system that dictated how they handled misbehavior. Now that they have to think for themselves, they're floundering. Could you send us a list of suggested techniques or consequences? I think it would help if they had a list to choose from."

Here is the list that I sent.

QUICK AND EASY
DISCIPLINARY INTERVENTIONS

Listed by degree of severity:

1. Give the student "the evil eye."

2. Walk toward the student.

3. Stand close to the student.

4. Make eye contact and a shake of the head indicating "No."

5. Place a gentle hand upon the shoulder of the student.

6. Make a statement indicating disfavor such as:
   "Really now, Jeff, must you?"
   "Just because I like you, should I let you get by with that?"

7. Change the student's location by asking:
   "Jeff, would you consider moving over here for a minute?"
   "Would you mind waiting here for a minute, and then we can talk?"

8. Make a statement indicating the behavior is just misplaced, such as:
   "That behavior would be fine on the playground. It isn't okay here."
   "That's not acceptable here."
   "Save it for later."

9. Use an "I" message:
   "I get distracted when there is a pencil tapping."
   "It scares me to see you running in the hall. Wait right here for a moment, then
   you can go."

10. Set limits by describing what you allow, do, or provide, without telling the students
    what to do about it:
    "I listen to people who raise their hands."
    "I give credit for all papers that are on my desk by 3:15."
    "I'll dismiss people as soon as desks are clean."
    "Feel free to return to the group as soon as you can handle it."

11. Provide choices:
    "Would you rather work quietly with the group or go to recovery?"
    "Would you rather talk this over quietly with me now or after school?"

12. Remove the student from the group to recovery. Student may return when he/she
    can live with the limitations of the group or teacher.

13. Provide the option for the student to fill in a form during time-out before he/she can
    return to the group:
    a. What happened?
    b. How did I feel?
    c. What did I do?
    d. How did it work?
    e. What am I going to do next time?

14. Excuse the student to the office for a short "cooling off" period. No counseling is requested of the administrator.

15. Give the student an appointment to talk about the problem. Counseling involves requiring him/her to come up with a new behavior before returning to the scene of the rule violation.

16. Restrict the student from the area of his/her infraction until a new plan of action is identified and written out by the student.

17. Restrict the student from the area of the infraction until the adults feel that another try is in order. The student then returns to the area on a day-to-day basis: "You may start using the playground again. Each good day you have earns you another day."

18. Provide a natural or logical consequence with empathy:
    "I'm sorry it worked out that way for you. Where are you going to eat now that you can't eat in the cafeteria? It has to be a place that won't be a problem for anyone else. Think it over and let me know."

19. Have the student make an "informational telephone call" to his/her parents to describe the problem and his/her plans for improvement. Teacher calls first without student's knowledge to alert parents and to seek support.

20. Have the student write an "informational letter" to his/her parents describing the actions or problem and his/her plans for improvement. Letter is to be signed and returned, and is the student's ticket to return to class.

21. Make an appointment with the administrator for consultation. The teacher, administrator, and student form a team to discuss possible solutions or consequences.

22. Hold a parent conference. This includes parent, teacher, administrator, and student.

23. Suspend the student from school until a parent conference is held.

24. Place the student on Systematic Suspension contract, being allowed to remain in school each day for as many minutes or hours as the child can live with an agreed-upon set of behavioral standards.

Training the Staff

Once the Core Beliefs document is developed and shared, it is time to train the staff. As tempting as it might be to train *all* teachers to use the Love and Logic techniques, this approach can become problematic. As the old saying goes, *"There are many ways to skin a cat."* I'm not sure where that saying comes from, but I'm sure it is a metaphor not having to do with a real cat.

Teachers appreciate working for a principal who acknowledges that there are many different and effective ways of working with kids. Remember that your goal is to get staff members to be consistent with the Core Beliefs. The goal is not to get them to become clones of each other.

It is helpful to say to the staff, "The Love and Logic training materials offer some very good techniques and ideas that are consistent with our Core Beliefs. We will offer a study group for those of you who are interested. We will use the *9 Essential Skills For The Love And Logic Classroom*®. I will be one of the participants in the class so I can learn with you."

The principal who is an active member of the study group sends a strong message about commitment and usually gets the most support from the staff in return. The principal who does not participate often sends an unstated message, "You guys are the ones who need to learn this, not me." I'm sure you've seen the negative morale problems, as well as a lack of buy-in from the staff, created by this lack of leadership.

The *9 Essential Skills* curriculum is designed so that it can be led by anyone who can follow the simple lesson plans. Increased staff buy-in often occurs when different staff members teach each module. Each month a different module is presented by a couple of staff members. Two teachers working as a team find this very easy.

"But what if a question comes up, and these people don't know the answer?" you ask. They shouldn't be expected to be the experts on the Love and Logic approach. They are only facilitating the presentation of the module. I once knew a teacher who responded to a difficult question with, "I don't know. I didn't write this program, but I know that the very fact that our school owns the program gives us the right to call Jim Fay directly. I'll do that and we'll see how he answers the question."

Our support is always available. Call 800.338.4065. *Consults with the authors are free to owners of this curriculum.*

Special reminders:

1. Make participation voluntary. Start out with the best teachers, not the ones that need rehabilitation. Let the others join later as they become interested.

2. Take it slow and easy. Don't teach more than one module at a time. Spread the study out over a period of time. This lets people experiment with the techniques and catch up with the paradigm shift.

3. Make it available to your support staff as well.

4. As the principal, plan to attend every session. Be a leader.

5. Remind staff that the Love and Logic approach is one way to become consistent with the Core Beliefs, but not the only way.

6. Have copies of the Love and Logic Institute's audio CD, *Quick and Easy Classroom Interventions*, available for staff to check out and review.

7. **Remind your staff that the Love and Logic way is not a discipline program, but instead, is a menu of techniques designed to make every thing else they do work better.**

I'm sure you've experienced new programs being introduced to teachers with the message, "Stop doing what you've been doing and do this instead." You've also witnessed the insecurity and problems this creates. It helps to give teachers frequent reminders that this is not the case as we evolve into a different school culture using Love and Logic skills.

An Effective Classroom

Thousands of teachers have heard of her. She's become famous, appearing in many of my stories about my own growth. She served as a mentor to me as I tried to give up my old ways of relying on fear to control or motivate students.

It's Mrs. Barlow, my friend and mentor. She ran a unique classroom. Her students were known to say, "Oh, Mrs. Barlow. She's really nice, but you don't want to mess with her."

"Oh, really? Why is that?"

"It would be really bad if you made trouble in the classroom or didn't do your work."

"Why?"

"Oh, she could do something awful."

"Oh, yeah? Have you ever seen her do awful things to kids?"

"No, but she really could, man."

I'd never heard of her having to use extreme measures on kids so I was baffled by this until I got to know her. I finally figured it out when she told me the secret to discipline.

"Jim," she said, "the secret to discipline is never let them see you sweat."

"What does that mean?"

"If you can handle difficult kids or difficult situations with a whisper, and you make it look really easy, the other kids will always suspect what you might be capable of if they actually make you mad. Many teachers do the right things but they make it look like their skills are maxed out. For some reason this causes the kids to test the teacher a lot more."
Her next piece of advice caught me by surprise.

Don't Show Your Hand (As they say in card games.)

"And Jim, it's a lot better if the kids don't know what kind of consequences you have in mind for their misbehavior. Don't let yourself get locked into anything you might want to change or can't do when they misbehave. Come visit my classroom and I'll show you how I get my discipline program started."

Presenting the Classroom Rules

I was fortunate to be in her classroom during first period as she introduced herself and her classroom rules.

"Well, kids. I don't have a lot of rules for the classroom. Here they are on this chart. There are only two of them."

She pointed to her rules chart.

1. Treat me with the same respect I treat you.
2. Don't make a problem.

"Now you are probably used to having a list of consequences for breaking rules, so you can see that on this other chart."

If you make a problem I will do something.

"The reason I do it this way is that every student is a unique and different person, and every problem is a unique and different problem. I don't treat everybody the same way. Why do you suppose that is, class?"

"'Cause we're all different?"

"You've got it kids. Pretty simple isn't it? Any questions?"

Here Came the Questions

"But what's a problem?"

"Oh, I bet you already know, but it's anything that makes it difficult for me to teach, other kids to learn, or kids to feel safe. I'll let you know if I see you making a problem so you can stop it before I have to do something."

"But what if you're not fair?"

"Oh, that could happen, especially if I don't have enough information about the situation, so here's what we'll do if that happens. Let's all practice saying these words, 'I'm not sure that's fair.' "

Mrs. Barlow had the kids practice this sentence over and over. She had them say it softly, faster, loudly, in a mean angry tone, and with whispering.

Once she completed this, she went over to her Consequence Chart and wrote, "If you can come to me and whisper, 'I'm not sure that's fair,' and present a good case with some new information, I'll change the consequence so it fits better."

She signed and dated the statement and turned to the class saying, "There. Now you have a written guarantee, signed and dated, that says that you can have a due process hearing. That's a legal term that means you get to have a chance to tell you side of the story. That doesn't always mean that you'll get your way, but if you can present a good case with new information, I'll do what? Class?"

The kids all chimed in with, "You'll change the consequence so it fits better."

"Bingo, and good luck. Now do you think that you can explain this to your parents?"

Dealing with a Parent Who Doesn't Understand This Approach to Discipline

It wasn't long before Mrs. Barlow had a chance to deal with a parent who complained that she should warn the kids in advance of their misbehavior.

"Travis doesn't get to sit with his friend anymore. And I don't think that's fair. All he was doing was trying to get some help. He wasn't just visiting. Besides, you don't have a rule about talking and you didn't tell him what was going to happen if he did. It's just not fair."

A calm and collected Mrs. Barlow sat back and answered, "I bet it looks that way. I'm glad you brought this to my attention. You're right that I don't have a specific rule about visiting while I'm instructing, and I don't tell kids exactly what I'm going to do. I try to treat all kids as unique individuals and each situation like a unique situation. My goal is to address each problem in a way that helps each individual kid grow and learn from his or her mistakes."

Mrs. Barlow went on, making the same explanation of her discipline approach that she delivered to the kids. She placed a lot of emphasis on her written guarantee of a due process hearing.

"Now Mom, I'm a little confused. I taught all the kids the right words to say and they rehearsed them with me. I gave them a written guarantee of being able to tell their side of the story. And I told them that if they could come up with a good case, I'd be glad to listen and possibly change the consequence. Now, based on all of that, why do you suppose he told you that I wasn't fair instead of coming to me? It seems like a bit of a slow way for him to get some help on this wouldn't you agree."

"Well, I don't know, I guess he just trusts me more than he does you."

"That could be true, and now Travis has two choices. He can come to me and present a good case, or maybe the two of you would like to present his side of the story. Please know that I am more than willing to listen and change the consequence if something else would help him learn about the right and wrong times to visit with his friend. Why don't the two of you talk it over and let me know."

This illustrates one of the benefits of setting up school and classroom discipline without locking into prescribed consequences. I guess that you quickly realized that very few parents went over this teacher's head with complaints to the principal.

I often ask parent audiences, "Would you rather have your children attend a school where every child is treated the same, or would you rather have them go to a school where children are treated as unique in-dividuals?" When I ask which of these schools they would best support, the answer is always the same. Parents are more willing to support those who treat their children as individuals.

Now, just for fun, with tongue planted firmly in my cheek, I'd like to ask if you know any schools that treat every child exactly the same. Do you know any schools that lie about it and claim that they do? Let's have a moment of silence as we ponder this weighty question.

Since those long ago days when Mrs. Barlow demonstrated this common sense way of running a classroom, thousands of teachers have heard me talk about it. Many have adopted and modified this method.

Sample Letter to Parents

Another very effective teacher, Amy Krochmal, put a new twist on it by creating a letter for parents that does an effective job of helping them understand why their children aren't in a typical classroom with typical rules and consequences.

Amy has released this letter for your use. You may use it as is, or modify it to fit your unique situation.

AN EXAMPLE LOVE AND LOGIC CLASSROOM DISCIPLINE PLAN:
A Letter Sent To Parents

Guidelines And Core Beliefs For Discipline
(Mrs. Krochmal 1996 – 1997)

Rules in my classroom are few. I believe that as all children are different, and all actions and reactions very personal in nature, effective discipline involves a few overriding tenets rather than a long list of specific rules. Situations are dealt with as they arise, with the focus on enabling the child to grow and learn from his or her actions.

Guidelines for student behavior:

1. You may engage in any behavior that does not create a problem for you or anyone else in the world.

2. If you find yourself with a problem, you may solve it by any means that does not cause a problem for anyone else in the world.

3. You may engage in any behavior that does not jeopardize the safety or learning of yourself or others. Unkind words and actions will not be tolerated.

In ensuring that the above guidelines are adhered to, I will operate with the following principles as my guide:

1. I will react without anger or haste to problem situations.

2. I will provide consequences that are not punitive but that allow the child to experience the results of a poor choice, enabling him or her to make better choices in the future.

3. I will proceed in all situations with the best interest of the whole child foremost in my mind. Academic, social, and emotional well-being will be fostered.

4. I will guide students toward personal responsibility and the decision-making skills they will need to function in the real world.

5. I will arrange consequences for problem situations in such a way that the child will not be humiliated or demeaned.

6. Equal is not always fair. Consequences will be designed to fit the problems of individual students, and they may be different even when problems appear to be the same.

7. I will make every effort to ensure that, in each situation, the students involved understand why they are involved in consequences.

8. If I at any time act or react in a way that a child truly feels is unjust, that student need only say to me, "I'm not sure that's fair." I will arrange a private conference during which the student can express to me why he or she feels my actions were not fair. This may or may not change my course of action. I am always open to calm, rational discussion of any matter.

Many teachers find that the following poster is very helpful:

HOW I RUN MY LOVE AND LOGIC CLASSROOM

1. I will treat you with respect, so you will know how to treat me.

2. Feel free to do anything that doesn't cause a problem for anyone else.

3. If you cause a problem, I will ask you to solve it.

4. If you can't solve the problem, or choose not to, I will do something.

5. What I do will depend on the special person and the special situation.

6. If you feel something is unfair, whisper to me, "I'm not sure that's fair," and we will talk.

©2005 Jim Fay & Charles Fay, Ph.D. Love and Logic Institute, Inc.
2207 Jackson Street, Golden, Colorado 80401-2300 ♥ 800-338-4065 ♥ www.loveandlogic.com

---

"But I Tried Those Techniques and They Don't Work"

Counseling With a Frustrated Teacher

Preparation for the Conference:

The Love and Logic approach offers an effective technique that works well with children and adults, alike. You will find it in the back of this book, titled, "Guiding Kids to Own and Solve Their Own Problems." Using this when counseling with teachers is a great opportunity to model the technique that you hope to see teachers using with the students.

Review the Six Reasons Why a Love and Logic Technique Might Not Work:

1. The adult displays anger or frustration.
2. The adult uses too many words or lectures.
3. The adult doesn't have a positive relationship with the child. (Gaining cooperation with someone who does not like you is seldom successful.)
4. The adult uses the wrong skill for the situation.
5. The child is mentally ill and needs professional help.
6. The adult uses warnings or threats.

Crucial Questions:
1. Which skill did you use?
2. How did you do it? This includes words, tone of voice, and body language.

Reminder:

A person is telling you nothing when he/she says, "I used the Love and Logic approach." Since the Love and Logic approach is only a menu of skills, it is important for them to be able to tell you which skill they used.

Sample Counseling Session between Principal and Teacher:

"I don't know what is wrong with that kid. Nothing works on him. I even used Love and Logic on him and he just ignored me. I was really close to giving him an office referral."

"Wow, that's no good. By the way, which technique did you use?"

"Well I used choices and he just kept being inappropriate."

"Well as you know, we're all learning this together, How about showing me exactly the way you did it with the exact words, tone of voice, and body language."

"Well, Jeff was chattering away with Ryan while I was teaching up front and I turned to him and gave him some choices."

"What were the choices?"

"I said, 'Are you going to settle down or am I going to have to send you to recovery?' "

"Were other kids able to hear what you said to him?"

"Well of course. I was in the front of the class."

"That helps me. Would you like to hear what some other teachers have tried with situations like that?"

"Oh, I guess so, but I don't know what's wrong with these kids these days."

"Some teachers check out this list of possible reasons a skill might not work. Here's the list:

1. The adult displays anger or frustration.
2. The adult uses too many words or lectures.

3. The adult doesn't have a positive relationship with the child.

4. The adult uses the wrong skill for the situation.

5. The child is mentally ill and needs professional help.

6. The adult uses warnings or threats.

"Some teachers check out the DVDs from the *9 Essential Skills for The Love And Logic Classroom* and review the modules.

"Some teachers check with others who've worked with Jeff to see what's worked for them. I've got some thoughts about the way you used the skill, would you be interested?"

"I'd be a lot more interested in you suspending him from school, but I guess . . . Oh, I guess I'd like your thoughts."

"I remember something in the *9 Essential Skills*, Module Number Seven, about choices; that choices don't work if they sound like threats. And I also remember Jim Fay writing that reprimanding a kid in front of other kids usually makes things a lot worse. You might want to experiment with whispering in his ear the next time.

"And by the way, have you experimented with the 'One Sentence Intervention' to get Jeff to really like you? That's another one of the skills from the Love and Logic curriculum. Kids who have a great relationship with their teachers are a lot more cooperative. You might want to give this all some thought and get back to me. Thanks for coming in.

"Oh, and remember that I'm more than happy to sit down with you and Jeff and see what else we can do together. If you'd like to do that, set up an appointment at your convenience."

Some interesting things happened during this conference:

1. The teacher didn't get to dump her responsibility on the principal.

2. The principal got better insight into the teacher's style.

3. The teacher received a message that she was responsible for changing her ways.

4. The principal was able to reinforce the importance of relationships.

5. The principal was able to reinforce the fact that he/she works with students only when the teacher is present.

CHAPTER II

Enforcing Consistency with Core Beliefs

I am writing this book for those of you are passionate about being a leader. There may be some principals who might want to put down this book now if they favor an approach dedicated to keeping every staff member happy. If that's not you, and you are willing to share your passion for developing a school that celebrates excellence, keep reading.

School principals who don't intend to hold teachers accountable for compliance with the Core Beliefs document should not waste their time going through the process of developing it.

Core Beliefs that are ignored are nothing more than "weasel words." We've all seen mission statements that are nothing more than an impressive collection of fancy words. These mission statements are less than worthless. In fact, mission statements that are ignored send a strong message that the manager or, in this case, the principal has neither the commitment nor tenacity to be the leader.

When this problem occurs in a business, morale problems build and infighting pits employees against each other and against the boss. Even while much of this is not overt, it still eats away at morale and coopera-tion. It is no different with the school staff.

Be the Leader

Your Core Beliefs document provides a very effective tool for establishing yourself as a positive and influential leader. This tool helps you to mandate consistency between teacher techniques and the Core Beliefs document without being seen as dictatorial. Positive professional relationships can be maintained and teachers can be held accountable for dealing with students in a manner consistent with the Core Beliefs document. This is the first of three important uses of this document.

I don't know many bosses who feel comfortable confronting an employee about substandard performance. It becomes even more uncomfortable when the time comes for the boss to write a letter of reprimand for the personnel file. Asking the employee to sign the letter prior to placing it in the personnel file is even more awkward. I was uneasy with this procedure throughout my entire career.

After 31 years in the school system, I left to open my own business. It took no time at all for me to find that I had the same problem. From time to time, I had to confront an employee about a performance issue and found that it was no easier in the private sector. When I tried to explain why the staff member's performance was unsatisfactory, I found myself on the defensive trying to justify my position.

Too often, it was easier to let poor performance slide than it was to face the issue. But now I had a bigger problem. The money that I lost from keeping a poor employee was my own money. Now let me tell you. That can become a motivator!

An Easy Solution

Desperate to find an answer, I hired a consultant company to work with me on this issue. The consultant identified the problem immediately. "Things are backward here," he offered. "The employee should be the one who has the job of convincing you that his/her performance is satisfactory. It should not be your job to convince the employee that his or her performance is substandard.

"Let that person prove to you that his/her performance is consistent with the company's mission statement. When it's the other way around you are letting the employee dictate the direction of the conversation. You tell the employee that something is wrong and then all he/she has to do is make excuses, which leads you to debate one "bird walk" after another. This is a lose/lose proposition."

Turn It Around:
Employ the *"Tell Me About It"* Strategy

The valuable advice he gave me was: "Here are your words, Jim. Say, 'I've noticed that you have been sounding impatient with customers on the phone. Tell me about that. Tell me how that's consistent with our mission statement.'

"Now the tables have been turned. It's time to sit back and let the employee do the convincing. You are in the control position. The monkey is now off of the boss's back and firmly stationed on the employee's back. You can either choose to be convinced or not. And I will guarantee you that this is a much more comfortable position to be in as a boss."

Armed with this new tool, I found myself feeling much more confident about confronting a staff member about performance. It was not long before I got to experiment with it, needing to address the performance of an employee who got her way too often by making those around her, including me "walk on eggshells."

I invited her into my office and said; "I've noticed when it's time for the staff to do the filing, you find other things to do, leaving the job for the others. Tell me about that. Tell me how that's consistent with the staff expectations."

I sat back and folded my arms and said nothing while she laid down one excuse after another.

"I'm confused," I replied. "I still don't get it. Tell me how it fits the job description."

I sat back and folded my arms while she gave it another try. Remaining unconvinced, I realized that I wasn't the one with the problem after all. It was kind of rewarding to be on the opposite side of a conversation like this. I was becoming excited about this technique.

The conversation ended with my asking her what we might expect in the future, and her saying that it wasn't fair for her to have to file, but that she would try to do better.

A week later she found herself in my office again, listening to me say, "Tell me about it."

The entire conversation was a repeat of her initial set of excuses, and my being confused. Several times I had to say, "But you're not telling me how it fits the job description. Tell me about that."

A week later, with her making no visible effort to improve, I invited her in to "Tell me about it." However, this time she was angry. "I don't have to put up with this! I quit!" My heart sang with the thought that since she had quit instead of being fired, we would not face any unemployment payments. Now I was sold on the "Tell me about that" approach.

A Principal Applys "Tell Me About That"

As principal Evelyn Davis walked passed room 217, she heard a teacher's voice raised to a fever pitch. Glancing into the room, she saw Martha standing over Glenn. Her finger was in his face as she was yelling, "I've had it with this non-sense! This is the third time this period that I've had to tell you to quit with the sarcastic remarks. The next time you open your mouth you are going to end up in in-school detention. Now I mean it this time!"

Resisting the temptation to step in and deal with the issue at the moment, Evelyn went back to her office to consider the best way of dealing with Martha's frequent yelling at students.

She thought to herself, "This has been going on for too long. I've had parent complaints about the way she relates to kids. Her students say that they hate her. She sends more kids to the office for discipline than any other teacher. And each time I try to talk to her about it she tells me that a little discipline doesn't hurt anyone. I don't know how many times she has complained that I'm not tough enough with the kids who come to the office for discipline."

Evelyn's staff had just completed the Core Beliefs document. Many of the staff members had been studying the *9 Essential Skills for the Love and Logic Classroom* curriculum and were experimenting with the techniques. As you can guess, Martha was not one of the teachers who volunteered for this.

"Now I have a better tool for dealing with Martha's negative approach," thought Evelyn.

The first of the staff's Core Beliefs was: "We will make every effort to maintain the dignity of both the student and the adult." "Now," thought Evelyn, "Martha's actions are a direct violation of the Core Beliefs. She was present at the meeting where these were developed, and I now have a specific behavior that I can address. I have a professional responsibility to deal with this issue."

Evelyn also had another new tool. She had learned about the "Tell me about that" technique. Her confidence was up and she had the tools to get the job done.

The Conference

"Martha, I asked you to come in to talk about our Core Beliefs. The first one on the list says that we will do everything we can to maintain the dignity of both the student and the adult.

"I watched you standing over Glenn with your finger in his face. You were yelling loud enough for me to easily hear all the way out into the hallway. Tell me about that. Tell me how that fits with the Core Beliefs."

"Well, Mrs. Davis. I've had it with that kid. Nothing works with him. If we had a little discipline around this school, he'd know that he couldn't act that way!"

"That might or might not be true, Martha, but you're not telling me how your actions fit our Core Beliefs."

"Well the big problem around here is that the other teachers don't enforce the rules the way they should. I'm the only one around here that expects kids to behave. If you did something about that, I'd have time to teach instead of constantly having to deal with disruptive behavior. How do you expect us to get any teaching done when we have to spend so much time on discipline?"

"I still don't get it, Martha. Tell me how yelling at him in front of the others fits our Core Beliefs."

"Well, I suppose it doesn't fit, but what am supposed to do?"

"Martha, would you like to hear what some of the other teachers are doing?"

"Well, maybe."

"They have been discovering some new techniques in a couple of places. Some of the teachers have been studying the Love and Logic curriculum, *9 Essential Skills for The Love And Logic Classroom*. Others have been listening to this audio CD, *Quick and Easy Classroom Interventions*. You can take it and see if there are some ideas that might help. I hope you find it useful, and let me know how I can help."

As Martha left the office, Evelyn thought to herself, "That went a lot better than I thought, but I know that Martha is not going to change over night. I'd better be prepared to have this conversation several times before she gets the message that I'm serious about all of us living with our Core Beliefs document."

It wasn't long before Evelyn had to repeat the "Tell me about that" conversation. Each time, Martha tried to place the blame on others but Evelyn didn't take the bait. Instead of debating Martha's accusations, she simply replied with, "But you're not telling me how that yelling and those threats fit our Core Beliefs."

During their third meeting, Martha went on the attack. "I don't know why you are on my case like this. You expect everyone to use those Love and Logic techniques, and I'm not sure I agree with them in the first place. I'm about ready to file a grievance with the teacher's association!"

"Martha, would you like my thoughts on this?"

"Oh, I guess so."

"First. I don't care which techniques you use, and I don't care where they come from. Find some that fit your personality, and as long as they don't violate our Core Beliefs, I'll support you.

"Second, you have yet to convince me that yelling and threatening are consistent with our Core Beliefs. And, third, you are within your rights to go to the teacher's association. Maybe someone there can convince me that your actions are consistent with our Core Beliefs."

Martha stomped out of the office muttering under her breath. As I think about this episode, it warms my heart to think:

1. The principal maintained a professional demeanor throughout.
2. Martha walked into each meeting with the monkey on her back and left each time with the monkey on her back.
3. The principal kept the conversations on a professional level rather than on a personal level.
4. Without attacking the teacher personally, she managed to get her to recognize that changes were going to have to be made.
5. This principal accomplished this by using two simple tools, The Core Beliefs document, and the "Tell me about that" approach.

After Martha's third encounter with the "Tell me about that" routine, she came to Evelyn and asked if she could join the group that was studying the *9 Essential Skills for the Love and Logic Classroom*. And with the help and support of a couple of other teachers she started making some progress.

At this point you may be thinking to yourself, "It's not always that easy." And you're right. Some teachers are so set in their ways that a stronger intervention is called for. That's the purpose of our next chapter.

The Teacher Who Is Not Good Enough to Keep, but Not Bad Enough to Fire

I once served as an expert witness in a trial where the school district was attempting to fire a teacher whose classroom methods had created many parent complaints about the anxiety she was creating for her young students. There had been many reports of the children having stomach aches, head aches, and sleeping problems. Yearly, a significant number of children had to be transferred to other classrooms because of doctor requests and demands from parents who reported that their kids were afraid to come to school.

The judge's ruling in this case was interesting. He ruled that the teacher's methods were detrimental to the emotional welfare of the children. He also ruled that he could not support the school district's hopes of firing the teacher. He based this decision on the fact that there was no paper trail showing that the teacher had been told that her actions were unprofessional. What a blow!

I left the courtroom trying to think of a way that this atrocity could have been avoided.

How could this have gone on for all this time? How many kids were damaged, or turned away from learning? No doubt, several different principals had tried in different ways to get her to change her ways.

Putting myself into this kind of situation, I could see how uncomfortable it is for a principal to write a formal letter of reprimand and ask a teacher to sign it. This is an easy thing to put off.

Going back to Martha's situation in Chapter Eleven, the monkey stayed firmly planted on her back because she was the one explaining her actions. The principal was reasonably comfortable in her position of either accepting or not accepting Martha's arguments.

Think about how much more comfortable it would be if the teacher wrote a document that served as a reprimand letter, signed it, and handed to you for your signature. What joy!

That is the purpose of the Professional Standards Incident Report. It can be used when staff members repeatedly violate the Core Beliefs without efforts to improve. On this form, the principal writes the section having to do with the observed actions of the teacher. The teacher fills in the next three sections. The document is signed and dated. One copy goes to the teacher. The other copy is filed in the teacher's personnel file. A paper trail is created.

If you would like to receive a free master copy of this form via email, contact us at the Love and Logic Institute, Inc. 800-338-4065.

PROFESSIONAL STANDARDS INCIDENT RECORD
Professional Staff Core Beliefs – Discipline

1. Every attempt will be made to maintain the dignity and self-respect of both the student and the teacher.
2. Students will be guided and expected to solve their problems without creating problems for anyone else.
3. Students will be given opportunities to make decisions and live with the consequences, be they good or bad.
4. Misbehavior will be handled with natural or logical consequences instead of punishment, whenever possible.
5. Misbehavior will be viewed as an opportunity for individual problem-solving and preparation for the real world as opposed to a personal attack on school or staff.
6. Students are encouraged to request a "due process hearing" whenever consequences appear to be unfair.
7. School problems will be handled by school personnel. Criminal activity will be referred to the proper authorities.

The above list of core beliefs outlines the professional actions and attitudes of all staff members in this school.

STUDENT DISCIPLINE INCIDENT CRITIQUE

Date of Incident: _____

Student's name(s):

_____
_____
_____
_____
_____
_____
_____

Staff member's name:

_____
_____
_____
_____
_____
_____

Supervisor's name:

_____
_____
_____
_____
_____
_____
_____

Supervisor's description of incident:

_____
_____
_____
_____
_____
_____
_____
_____
_____
_____
_____
_____

Staff member, please describe in your own words how your actions and/or attitudes in this incident are consistent with our Professional Staff Core Beliefs:

_____
_____
_____
_____
_____
_____
_____
_____
_____
_____
_____
_____
_____
_____

Staff member, please describe in your own words what can be expected of you in the future:

_____

_____

_____

_____

_____

_____

_____

_____

_____

_____

_____

_____

Staff member, if changes in performance require additional training, what kind of support would you like to see from administration?

_____

_____

_____

_____

_____

_____

_____

_____

_____

_____

_____

Staff member's signature: _____

Date: _____

Motivating Negative Teachers to Become the Teachers We'd Like Them to Be

This is another opportunity to put the Core Beliefs document into use. It should be the job of these teachers to convince you that their actions or techniques are consistent with the Core Beliefs document. Before doing so, you might want to consider the following thoughts:

One day I got a call from a principal. "Jim, thanks for taking my call. I'd love to hire you to speak to my staff. I have a few negative teachers who don't believe in treating kids with dignity. I'm afraid that they've never heard the word empathy. I cringe every time I think about how they treat kids. I've heard that Love and Logic training actually causes many teachers to change their styles. That's exactly what we need. I thought that our school would work a lot better if those teachers could feel more positive."

"Wow," I replied. "Thanks for the good thoughts, but I wouldn't be interested in coming to any school to help negative teachers feel better about themselves. If that were the intent of my presentation, it would be difficult thing to disguise. I'm sure you know how that works. Once your unstated message indicates that a person doesn't measure up, defense mechanisms leap into action, and you get the opposite results.

"Now, if you'd like me to make a presentation that would help all of your positive teachers feel better about what they are doing, and help the negative ones feel left out, possibly motivating them to either change or find a different profession, I'd be more than happy to do that."

"Well, let's do that, but I need some strategies for dealing with these teachers who are so negative with the kids."

Positive teachers should get our professional services as well as our emotional energies. Negative teachers should get our professional services only.

This statement does not indicate that we give up on negative teachers. Our job as principals is to help them become more effective. I have seen too many situations in which a principal spends so much emotional energy on helping substandard teachers feel good about themselves that the good teachers get left out. When I've asked these principals how their efforts have paid off, they just sigh. How many positive strides do you think might have happened if that same emotional energy had been given to the positive teachers instead?

You might think about it in these terms. Suppose you want to change a community. Would it be most effective to identify all of the most dysfunctional families and put your emotional resources into changing them, or would it be most effective to put those same resources into the more functional families while still providing service to those in need? You're right. It is very unlikely that those dysfunctional families are going to make many changes. History gives us the answer to this question. We've all watched our government struggle with this same issue.

A school is just a smaller community. Best results come from putting our emotional resources into those staff members who are both anxious and willing to grow. They are our change agents. At the same time, we hold teachers accountable for being consistent with the Core Beliefs document, and provide pressure as well as opportunities for them to grow.

Negative teachers should not feel comfortable with their teaching styles.

Schools should not serve as rehabilitation centers for teachers whose personal or professional problems cause them to resist using positive methods.

SPECIAL NOTE: It is important to remember that many teachers who have difficulty working with children are often good people who have found themselves in the wrong profession. It is still important that they get the same respect we afford children. Notice their strengths while at the same time being honest about whether or not their skills and actions support the Core Beliefs document. The One Sentence Intervention, found in Module Five in the *9 Essential Skills for the Love and Logic Classroom®*, is a powerful tool for accomplishing this. Use of this skill is a great way to model for teachers.

Additional Uses for the Core Beliefs Document

Core Beliefs Document Use #1: Holding Teachers Accountable for the Positive Teacher-Student Interactions

Chapter Eight addressed the issue of holding teachers and other staff members accountable for their actions. In most cases principal/teacher conferences employing the "Tell me how it fits" technique is a very effective way of bringing teachers into compliance with the school's Core Beliefs.

Knowing that, from time to time, there are teachers who either can't or won't buy into treating kids in accordance with the Core Beliefs, you may be forced to document their behaviors.

Use of The Professional Standards Incident Records Form in Chapter Eight will help you make a bold statement about your own commitment to the Core Beliefs document. At the same time, it can provide a written record that can be used in other ways if necessary. My experience has shown that the use of this form gets the attention of teachers in short order. Some teachers make efforts to upgrade their skills while others seek a transfer to another building where expectations might be a little less demanding.

Core Belief Document Use #2: Informing the Community

Now that you have developed the Core Beliefs document, it's time to share it with your community. It will serve as a bold and positive statement about how teachers interact with students.

My experience has shown that this kind of information is comforting to parents who don't have a clear picture of the positive changes that have occurred in schools since the days when they were students. It's reassuring for parents to know that their sons or daughters will be treated as unique individuals. Parents who know that their educators have an actual code of ethics are less critical and more supportive than those who are not sure about how the teachers deal with their children.

Please don't feel locked into labeling this document as Core Beliefs. I've see schools title it in different ways. Here are some of the titles I have seen:

Our Code of Ethics
Our Disciplinary Code of Ethics
Our Staff Code of Ethics
Our Guiding Principles
Our Commitment
Our Core Beliefs
Our Guiding Lights

One principal introduced this to the community with the following lead statement on the front page of the school-wide discipline policy. Feel free to copy this or modify it to fit your unique situation.

Dear Parents,

All of our students here at Lake View Middle School are unique individuals with unique personalities, talents, strengths, weaknesses, and needs. In the past, we have tried to fit these individual traits into a discipline system where every discipline problem was treated the same way in accordance with prescribed consequences. The results have not always met the unique needs of individual children.

In the process of developing a new discipline policy, the staff has prepared a set of beliefs that will be known as our Code of Ethics. This Code of Ethics will serve as our guide for dealing with student discipline problems.

Every attempt will be made to deal with students in accordance with this Code of Ethics. Please understand that we might slip from time to time. If you notice us dealing in ways that are inconsistent with our Code of Ethics, please bring it to our attention. We will thank you for that and attempt to make things right.

LAKE VIEW MIDDLE SCHOOL
CORE BELIEFS

This list of core beliefs outlines the professional actions and attitudes of all staff members in this school.

1. Every attempt will be made to maintain the dignity and self-respect of both the student and the teacher.
2. Students will be guided and expected to solve their problems without creating problems for anyone else.
3. Students will be given opportunities to make decisions and live with the consequences, be they good or bad.
4. Misbehavior will be handled with natural or logical consequences instead of punishment, whenever possible.
5. Misbehavior will be viewed as an opportunity for individual problem-solving and preparation for the real world as opposed to a personal attack on school or staff.
6. Students are encouraged to request a "due process hearing" whenever consequences appear to be unfair.
7. School problems will be handled by school personnel. Criminal activity will be referred to the proper authorities.

NOTE: This list represents a typical consensus when teachers and administrators examine their goals and working with school discipline problems.

Core Beliefs Document Use #3: Conferencing with Parents

When a parent-teacher conference goes bad, where does it end up? Right in your lap, right? Who is caught right in the middle of a rift? You, right? Who ends up trying to pick up the pieces? You, right?

These kinds of situations can go poorly for even the best of educators who are trying to do the right things. Consider the following parent-teacher interaction.

Troy's mom, Mrs. Jamison, is upset about the fact that Mrs. Jenkins confiscated her son's cell phone.

"Mrs. Jenkins, it's about time you quit picking on my son. You never see what the other kids are doing. I don't know what you have against him. This thing with his cell phone is the last straw. All he was doing was trying to change it to his other pocket and you took it away for no reason. How is he supposed to respect teachers when you are so unfair?"

"He wasn't just moving the phone. He was texting, and he knows that using the phone in class is against the rules."

"No, he wasn't. I asked him and he said that he wasn't. My boy doesn't lie."

"Maybe you don't know him as well as you think. I stood behind him, watching, and he was using his phone to get the answers for the test."

"You had no business looking at his phone for that. That violates his privacy. He has rights. Besides, he says that you never take phones from your pets. They get by with everything. I don't know why you don't like him."

"I do like him, but I have to enforce the rules, and there is a rule about using phones during class time."

"Well I can see that you don't want to listen. I'm taking this to the principal."

Now the Problem Is in the Principal's Lap

"I'm sorry to have to bother you with this," says Troy's mom. "But his teacher is totally unreasonable. She took Troy's phone for no reason."

"Wow! That's got to be upsetting. I need to hear more about that. Before I do, I'm wondering if you'd be willing to review our Core Beliefs document with me. We recognize that every child and every situation in this school is unique, so we use this document as our guide."

Create a Point of Common Agreement

"Mrs. Jamison, do you see anything in our Core Beliefs document that you disagree with? If not, can we agree that this unique situation needs a unique resolution that does not violate the principles in our Core Beliefs document?"

"No. I like these. I don't want him treated like he's just a number here, but I expect him to get treated fairly. I don't understand why his teacher picks on him like she does."

"Well, Mrs. Jenkins, now I need to hear about this. Tell me what you know."

At his point the wise principal listens, takes notes, and allows the parent to vent her frustrations. However, it is a grave mistake to render any final decisions during this session.

The eventual solution is best made with all parties involved: the parent, the student, the teacher, and the principal.

Get Everybody Together

"Mrs. Jenkins, I need to schedule a meeting where we can all look at this problem together."

The principal has paved the way for a more successful conference by being a good listener, giving Mrs. Jenkins a chance to vent her frustrations, and gaining common agreement through use of the Core Beliefs document.

The next step in a successful resolution involves the use of a four-step process for dealing with people who are angry, intimidating, or difficult. This will be presented later in this book. Had the teacher known and applied this technique, it is unlikely that this problem would have landed in the principal's lap.

Core Beliefs Document Use #4: Staff Hiring

Your Core Beliefs document can be a powerful tool for identifying and hiring staff members who are consistent with your school's Core Beliefs. Prior to interviewing a prospective teacher, provide a copy of the worksheet, "Creating Your School's Core Beliefs." Ask the applicant to pick five to six beliefs that best describe his/her own beliefs about working with students regarding discipline.

What often happens here is that the applicant goes to work thinking, "How can I answer these so that they will be consistent with the principal's belief system?"

During the interview, go over the applicant's answers.

"I see that you chose numbers 1,5,7,8, and 13. Let's go over those one at a time. I'd like for you to tell me the techniques you use to support these and make them happen."

The teacher you are looking for will be able to give you some practical techniques and will have little trouble discussing these beliefs. This person has based his/her answers on personal beliefs and experience. The other teachers will flounder. Use of this document raises the odds of your finding teachers who will fit into your school's culture.

Evolutionary, Not Revolutionary Changes

One year, long ago, I learned a tough but important lesson that made me decide to change my teaching style. Attempting to use fear as both a motivator and discipline tool during my early career created more problems for me than it solved. It all blew up the day that my frustration got the better of me and I slapped one of my students.

You're probably wondering how I managed to stay in the profession. Had that happened today instead of the year 1968, I would've been ousted immediately. Another thing that saved me was that I had a good relationship with the child's mother, who was no less frustrated than I was.

Hurt and embarrassed, I decided that I was going to give up my old techniques of intimidation and coercion and become a nice teacher. I soon found out that I had a bigger problem. I was too afraid to use my old ways, but had nothing to replace them with. The result: I lost control of my classroom and didn't get it back for a quite a while.

My teaching style change could've been far less painful and more effective had someone told me to not make any drastic changes until I had experimented with, and mastered, some new skills first. I hope you will encourage your teachers to move slowly into their new styles.

Invite Teachers to Experiment Before Changing

The Love and Logic Curriculum, *9 Essential Skills for The Love and Logic Classroom*, offers these skills. The wise principal introduces these skills one at a time, by providing the class once or twice per month on a voluntary basis.

Our experience tells us that some teachers, often those who need it the most, find the paradigm shift too challenging when they are asked to learn more than a couple of skills during a setting. However, it seems to work out well for them to ease into the program by learning and experimenting with one skill at a time.

Don't Ask Them to Throw Away Their Security Blankets

Emphasize that the teachers should experiment with each new skill and then decide for themselves whether or not to blend it into their repertoire. Those who have been most successful mastering the Love and Logic skills have taken them one at a time, gradually modifying them to fit their own individual personalities. Teachers are most secure about this when they're not asked to stop doing what they are used to and start out on a new path with new and different skills.

Frequently remind teachers that the Love and Logic approach is a menu of skills designed to make everything else they do work better. It is not a step-by-step discipline program.

Let your new school culture evolve gradually.

Lasting reform seldom comes through revolution.

Creating a Love and Logic school is not a school overhaul

Many years ago, I had the honor of consulting with Dr. Betsy Geddes, who was a principal at the time. She had just taken over an inner city school in Portland, Oregon. The school was out of control. Roving gangs of kids walked the halls screaming at teachers. Teachers were yelling at kids. I was hard-pressed to see how much learning could take place.

Three years later the school was much calmer. The change was obvious. The teachers were no longer yelling at kids. There were smiles on the faces of the students. Those teachers who had not yet bought into the new approaches were feeling in the minority.

Dr. Geddes had worked a miracle. The process she used to accomplish this is the one you have been reading about in this book. Granted, this process has been tweaked and refined over the years, as it will be in the future, as we continue our quest to make it easier to understand and implement.

As this process continues to evolve, you and many other leaders will be creating schools where teachers love to teach and kids love to learn the Love and Logic way.

When Consequences Don't Work

Ask Yourself:

1. Did I implement the consequence with compassion?
If not, the child becomes focused upon my emotions rather than his/her problem.

2. Was I in the emotional state when I implemented the consequence?
If I was, the child becomes focused upon my emotions rather than on his/her problem.

3. Did I deliver the consequence in a questioning manner?
"Where are you going to eat now that you can't use the cafeteria?"

4. Did I try to reason with the child while he/she was still in the emotional state?
Never attempt to reason with a child who is in the emotional state. It is a waste of energy and usually results in a power struggle.

5. Did I tie the time and location of the violation to the consequence?
The consequence has to be reasonable in the mind of the child. If not, it feels like retaliation to the child.

6. Did I use the consequence to get even with the child?
We cannot hide our intentions from children. This will cause resentment. As a result, the consequence loses its value.

7. Did I use a consequence when a disciplinary intervention would have solved the problem and allowed me to keep teaching?
Save consequences for the big lessons children need. Use the Quick and Easy Classroom Interventions to break the emotional spell whenever you can.

8. Did my attitude or behavior indicate to the child that I was trying to teach him/her a lesson?
We can't hide our attitudes from children. If they think we are implementing consequences to teach them lessons, they spend their time trying to show us that it won't work.

9. Did I implement the consequence immediately?
Delayed consequences are usually much more effective than immediate ones. Take your time, talk it over with friends and deliver the consequence when both you and the student are in the thinking state.

10. Did I tell the child in advance, what the consequence would be?
This is not effective. Kids either decide the consequence is worth it, or sometimes act out to see if the adult means what he/she says.

REMEMBER: There are a limited number of children who have not yet developed cause and effect thinking. These kids often do not have an internalized conscience. They still need to experience the consequences on a consistent basis. The results are not lessons may not be learned by the child, but serve as protection for the other children and the teacher.

Success with Difficult Parent Teacher Conferences

Expectant mothers, Tess and Maria, visited over lunch about their new babies and their dreams for them.

"You, know, Tess, I'm hoping to have an unhappy child, one that struggles in school, hates his teachers, ends up in special education, and just becomes a burden to my husband and me."

"Those are pretty good dreams, Maria, but I've got better dreams for my kid. I'm hoping that he's defiant and hates authority. I want him to be the kid who'd rather make the kids in the classroom laugh instead of doing his schoolwork. Maybe he can drop out of school, have several failed marriages, and do some hard time in prison along the way."

Absurd! This conversation never took place. And I've never known parents who had a written plan for their children's failure.

Parents, generally, have a different set of dreams. They dream that their kids will be happy, have friends, be successful in life, and be a blessing to the family, etc.

School Problems Herald the Shattering of Dreams

School problems herald the shattering of these dreams and many parents feel a sense of loss and grief. As we all know, people handle grief and loss in many different ways.

One wise principal discovered this after a year of trying to make accommodations for parents of his special education preschool program. Visiting with me he said, "I have 750 kids in my school and only 40 of them are in the special education preschool. Can you believe that I've spent 85 percent of my time dealing with the parents of the special education program?

"It doesn't seem to matter what I do for them. They demand all kinds of accommodations for their kids, and even if I provide what they want, they are still unhappy. Not only do these conferences burn up a lot of time, the parent demands are often interventions that will do more harm than good. I need to find a different way to deal with these parents."

As we visited about the possibility of shattered dreams for the parents of special education students, he exclaimed, "I bet that's it. I bet these parents are going through the stages of loss and grief. That's what I should have been addressing instead of focusing on the merits of their demands."

He continued with, "I know the stages of loss and grief. The first stage is denial. That's what the demands are all about. If they can just get a different accommodation for their child, then he/she doesn't really have the problem and their dream is not shattered after all. I just have to figure out a way to get these parents out of denial."

Stopping short, he said, "No, maybe that's not so good. The second stage is anger. I may not be ready for that!"

As he pondered the situation, a plan was being formulated. He went on to talk about ways of helping people who are suffering loss and grief.

Treating Loss and Grief

Grief counselors teach us that the following does little to help a person recover from loss and grief:

- Telling a person to look on the bright side
- Telling a person that time will heal the hurt
- Telling a person that he/she is strong and will be able to weather the storm
- Reasoning with a person about his/her complaints
- Telling a person to toughen up
- Making special accommodations

The most helpful treatment is getting or allowing someone to talk about his/her disappointment, pain, feelings, etc. The more a person talks with an empathetic and understanding person the better it is.

This wise principal decided that he needed to find ways to get parents talking about their shattered dreams before dealing with their demands.

One year later, I got a call from him. He was exuberant. "Jim, I had a much better year. My conferences were much more congenial. I spent a lot more time in each conference dealing with the loss and grief issue, but I had a lot fewer conferences over all. I got more support from the parents, and I think we did a better job of addressing the needs of these kids."

Step-By-Step Process for Dealing With A Difficult Parent

There are three things that we typically do, that sabotage our best efforts to maintain a win/win parent conference:

1. Defending
2. Explaining
3. Reasoning

There is a time and a place for these actions. However, that time comes after we have helped a parent move out of the emotional state. It is a rare to find a parent who comes to school with concerns, demands, complaints, etc., who is not in the emotional state at some level. Concerned parents are talking about their most cherished possession, their child. These parents are talking about a situation that has the potential to shatter their dreams for their youngster. You can bet your last dollar that these parents are in the emotional state.

People who are in the emotional state are not listeners. Any attempt to defend, explain, or reason is not only going to fall on deaf ears, but will most likely make them more upset and emotional.

Gently Move Parents Out of the "Emotional State" and Into the "Thinking State"

We cannot move people from the emotional state to the thinking state. They do this for themselves with our help. The only way I know how to do this is with words. Not my words, their words.

Don't Paraphrase

I am not talking about a counseling session where you apply your paraphrasing skills. This is a different set of skills that give parents the opportunity to use and hear back their own exact words and feelings about the situation. In the process, they actually bring themselves out of the emotional state.

Step One: Collect Information

"This must be upsetting. Tell me more."

Your job at this point is to ask as many pertinent questions as possible without reacting. Remember, no defending, reasoning, or explaining. This is strictly a collection of information. Ask if it's okay to take some notes.

Examples:

- How did you learn about this?
- When did you learn about this?
- Have you talked with anyone else about it?
- What was your reaction?
- What does you child say about this?
- What are your feelings about this?
- Has this kind of thing happened in the past?
- How are you hoping to resolve this?

NOTE: Taking notes, stopping the parent from time to time to allow you to catch up and be accurate, serves several purposes. It shows that you are serious about understanding and it slows down the parent, often having a calming effect.

End this step with, "Is there anything else that you can think of, or need me to understand?"

Step Two: Prove That You've Heard Everything

"Let's see if I've got it."

Read or say the parent's words back to them as accurately as possible. Remember, no paraphrasing.

Examples:

- You're saying that I don't like your child.
- You're saying that it's not his fault.
- You're saying that I pick on him.
- You're saying that the other kids cause him to get into trouble.
- You're saying that the other kids get preferential treatment.
- You're saying that I have no business running a school.

After you have repeated the parent's words, ask, "Is there anything that I've missed?" Notice that it is still not time to react to the information that you've collected.

Step Three: Check for the Parent's Entry Into the Thinking State

"Would you like my thoughts?"

This is a very effective way to see if the parents have actually left the emotional state and are ready to listen. If the parent says that he/she would like your thoughts, it is now possible to move on toward problem solving. If the parent says, "No," it is time to go back to the first step and collect more information, and, of course, prove that you've heard it.

"It looks like I haven't heard everything you need to tell me. Tell me about that."

Step Four: Problem Solving

The parent is now in the thinking state and asking for your thoughts. You're on your way to a win/win solution.

Hopefully, you have created the school's, Core Belief document. It will be helpful to share this with the parent and get common agreement that situations are treated on a case-by-case basis.

"Before I share my thoughts on this matter, here are our Core Beliefs. They serve as a Code of Ethics for us. Would you mind reading through them and see if there's anything you disagree with before we move on to finding a solution?

"We're going to try to find a solution that does not violate any of these Core Beliefs. If, by chance, I suggest anything that does violate these, I'd appreciate your letting me know."

Now it is time to start the problem solving process. And once more, we find a valuable use for the Core Beliefs document.

The rest of this book includes a variety of information about the use of the Love and Logic menu of skills plus some unique application of these skills. I hope you find it a valuable resource.

One More Reminder

Schools that own Love and Logic Curricula, have direct access to the authors. We are only a phone call away when you need assistance with implementation.

Success with Repeat Offenders

The search for the Holy Grail of education, in other words, the discovery of that single technique that would put a stop to that repeat offender's disruptive behavior, has tormented the minds of great educators for years. Educators have experimented with techniques including threats, lectures, punishment, in-school suspension, detention, demerit systems, token economies, rewards, and outright bribes. Each year the latest panacea is launched with great promise. If you look back over the years, you will probably recognize that each of these programs is a slightly different version of an earlier token economy. Usually only the words and rewards are different.

Just think, if any expert could discover that single technique he/she would be, by far, the most highly decorated educational consultant of all time. That person would be a shoe-in for induction into the Educators Hall of Fame.

After fifty-some years of searching, I have to admit that there is no single technique that will change the behavior of every repeat offender of school rules. Having given up the search for that single technique, I found that there are some techniques that help raise the odds of being successful with kids who don't respond to typical disciplinary interventions.

There are techniques that help prevent many of the disruptive behaviors of repeat offenders. These techniques and skills help teachers reduce the number of discipline problems they experience each day so that they have time and energy to manage the ones they are forced to deal with. For many years, the Love and Logic skills that focus on building positive relationships and preventing problems have proven to be highly effective tools for dealing with repeat offenders.

But Why Is It So Difficult to Reach These Kids?

It's human nature to look for a single reason for our problems. Our brains are driven to achieve closure so that we can feel a sense of control and security. Our human brains do not like to feel conflicted. As a result, it's normal for us to jump to conclusions about why kids are misbehaving. It helps us feel secure to think and then lock in on reasons such as: the kid just doesn't care, is looking for attention, is just trying to make me mad, is running with the wrong crowd, or has a bad home life. Once that happens we fixate on finding that single technique that will cure the problem.

However, there are as many different reasons for kids being repeat offenders as there are repeat offenders. Of course, this list could go on and on. However here are a few of the reasons:

1. The student feels that he/she has no relationship or a bad relationship with the teacher. Kids who hate their teachers don't respond to consequences. It's easy for them to think, "I don't like that teacher. Why should I do anything for him/her?"
2. The student misbehaves to cover up for a belief that he/she can't do the assignments as well as the other students.
3. The student has found that there is more pride in acting out or refusing than having to admit that he/she can't do the work.
4. The student may believe that acting out is the only way to be part of his/her chosen peer group.
5. The student may be paying the teacher back for perceived injustices or embarrassment.
6. The student believes that the school's treatment or discipline is an attempt to "teach him/her a lesson" or get even with him or her. Kids who develop this belief would rather face harsher discipline than feel like they are losing a battle.
7. The teacher shows frustration or anger while dealing with the student. This invariably brings out the worst in kids.
8. The student is facing a difficult situation at home and dealing with this, even on a subconscious level, raises his/her arousal level.
9. The teacher uses warnings and threats. This only works on the kids who are going to behave in the first place.
10. The home may be giving the student negative messages about the school and the teacher.

11. The student has severe self-concept issues.

12. The teacher calls out the student's name or directs him/her loudly enough that others hear, creating embarrassment. Teachers who whisper to kids have far fewer problems than those who talk to kids from across the room.

13. The student has been conditioned through systematic desensitization to require increasingly harsher consequences. This can happen when schools apply typical progressive discipline plans in which each offense earns a more severe intervention. The classic example of this is about the frog in a pot of cool water that gradually heats until it eventually boils the frog. The frog doesn't jump out of the water, but if you put him in hot water he would immediately jump out.

14. The student may have significant emotional problems and is need of professional help.

15. The student views the world as a win/lose place. Instigating, and winning power struggles, has become a way of life.

16. The student's basic human needs for physical and emotional security, love and affection, healthy, control, and a sense of inclusion are not being met.

What Does Ancestry Have to Do With Repeat Offenders?

One of the basic temperaments we are all born with has to do with how we see the world. Some kids are born predisposed to see the world as a win/win place. They tend to think to themselves, "If I do what others want me to do, they will win and so will I. The world is a good place for me."

Other kids are born predisposed to see the world as a win/lose place. They tend to think to themselves, "If I do what others tell me to do, they are going to win and I am going to lose. I better not let this happen."

This child will have experienced, and probably won, many power struggles with his/her parents before ever entering school. By this age, the child has already been developing and honing his/her resistive skills to an art form. Instigating, and winning power struggles, has become a way of life. Upon entering school, this win/lose view of life has intensified and teachers are going to find this child a challenge.

There are many variations within the win/win and win/lose views of life. Genetics and home life both play a part in determining how strong or weak this temperament becomes. I'm sure that you have already guessed which view of life produces the most repeat offenders.

Raising the Odds for Success

The odds for success with repeat offenders increase when we apply a number of strategies and skills. As you study the Love and Logic approach, it will become obvious that the skills are designed to meet basic human needs. People tend to gravitate toward and build relationships with others who help them meet those needs.

First and foremost, repair the teacher-pupil relationship. Perfectly designed consequences have little effect when the child either dislikes the teacher or believes that the teacher dislikes him/her.

Apply the "One Sentence Intervention." View the video presentation in Module Five in the *9 Essential Skills for the Love and Logic Classroom*® curriculum for a better understanding.

Do not assume that the pupil-teacher relationship is solid. One way to be sure is to whisper to the student from time to time, "Will you stop doing that just for me." Until that question is answered in the positive, the relationship is probably still strained.

Greet all students at the door each day with a smile and a handshake instead of a stern look. Teachers who do this seem to have fewer problems and higher success with difficult kids. In spite of what tough kids act like, they still gravitate toward teachers who greet them, act as if they're glad to see them, and thank them for coming to school.

Focus on preventing misbehavior to avoid needing to discipline or consequence bad behavior. Save consequences for the serious infractions where an important life lesson needs to be learned. Module Eight in the *9 Essential Skills* curriculum provides a variety of techniques to help teachers squelch bad behavior before it gets out of hand. This often can be done without interfering with instruction. An example would be whispering in the ear of a kid who is just starting to visit with his friend, "Oh, Jason, could you save that for Mr. Field's class? Thank you." Then walk away without looking back. Find a list of these on page 35. Delay consequences until the adults have had time to cool down and brainstorm the best possible consequence.

Tie consequences to the time or the place of the infraction instead of picking a consequence from a sequential list. Take time to ask, "What would happen to an adult in the real world who did that?" Kids are able to live with consequences better when they can make a connection between their behavior and the consequence. Kids have often said to me, "I don't mind having to live with consequences as long as the adult doesn't rub salt in the wound by lecturing or telling me what I'm suppose to learn from the situation."

Preface consequences with sincere empathy. Empathy changes brain chemistry, activating the frontal cortex, thus putting the student into the thinking mode instead of the fight-or-flight mode. Leading with empathy makes it much more difficult for the child to see the adults as being either mean or the source of the problem. An example would be, "Oh, wow. This is sad. Swearing at the bus driver. What's your plan for getting to school for the next three days? Do you need any help explaining this to your parents?"

Don't become a hostage to a discipline plan that spells out consequences in advance. These typical plans give too much power to the repeat offender. Kids like this conduct a cost/benefit analysis. "Let's see. If I do this, the adults are going to do that. Is it worth it? Yeah, I think it is." It is far better to state expectations and let kids know that if rules are broken, we will do something that seems appropriate to us at the time.

Replace in-school suspension with the recovery process offered in Module Four of the Love and Logic curriculum. You will find more about it on page 97 of this book. All students should understand that they are welcome in the classroom for every minute in which they do not cause a problem for the teacher or their classmates. Bad minutes can be spent in "recovery." They are welcome back to class as soon as they can be there without making it difficult for the teacher to teach or others to learn.

Students That Feed Off Each Other

If children are going to survive and thrive in tomorrow's complex world, they need practice solving as many problems as possible—today! The following process is designed to get kids thinking more about their problems than we do.

1. **Make a list of the students involved.**
2. **Prioritize the list.**
   The most compliant student is at the top of the list and the least compliant student is at the bottom of the list.
3. **Divide and conquer**
   Arrange with fellow teachers to provide a chair in the rear of their classrooms so that you can send the students, one at a time, to separate classrooms to sit and think about their behavior. You will need one room for each student. Your student will not be expected to participate with the other class. Each student goes with the understanding that he/she may return to class when that will not result in any form of disruption.
4. **Meet with the principal to describe your solution and ask for support.**
   "I am doing this because I can't allow these children to continue to disrupt the class. I don't want to make a problem for you, so if any one of these students acts out in the temporary classroom, I'd like him/her to come to you for a 'cool down' period. Please don't feel a need to do anything other than allow the student to cool down and then return to my class."
5. **When the disruption starts:**
   You have two options, depending on the strength of the leader of the group. In the event that you can move the group leader out to another location, do that first and say to the other group members "Do you guys think you can get yourselves back together, or do I need to find another place for you?"

In the event that you question the ease with which you can remove the leader, follow this plan:

    a. Go to the first student (most compliant) on the list and say "That is not acceptable. Mr. Sawyer has a place in his room for you until you can get yourself back together. You may return when you know that you can be here without causing a problem. Thank you."

    b. As soon as this one has left the room, go to the next student on the list and say, "Mrs. Babcock is expecting you in her room. You may return as soon as you can be here without causing a problem. Thank you."

    c. Continue this process until you get to the last student (least compliant) and say, "Now, do you think you can behave here or would you rather go to a different room until you can? Thank you."

You might find it helpful to send another student to make sure that the individuals have gone to their assigned rooms.

6. Implement the "One Sentence Intervention" with the children who are troublemakers.

7. Start having "heart to heart" talks with these students after school. Meet with them one at a time. The idea here is not to solve the problem all at one sitting, but to plant some seeds of thought in the student's mind.

> **TEACHER:** "Jeremy, I noticed that you are having a hard time behaving when you are around your friends. Are you aware that it makes it hard for me to teach when that's happening?"
>
> **JEREMY:** "I guess."
>
> **TEACHER:** "There are several different reasons why this happens with some kids. Sometimes it's because they hate the teacher, sometimes they are afraid that the work is too hard, sometimes it's because the kids are part of organized crime, sometimes it's because things aren't going well at home, and sometimes it's because the kids need friends so badly that they are willing to act out in class to be part of a group. Does anything sound familiar to you?"
>
> **JEREMY:** "I don't know."

TEACHER: "Well, that's sad not to know. Thanks for giving it some thought. I'll see you."

TEACHER: "Oh, by the way, do you think this behavior is going to change by tomorrow?"

JEREMY: "Yeah, I guess."

TEACHER: "Thanks Jeremy, I'm sure that would be best for all of us."

Continue the heart to heart talks until a better relationship is developed between the teacher and the student. In the event that things are not better the next day, the following conversation may be helpful.

TEACHER: "Guess what this looks like to me?"

JEREMY: "I don't know."

TEACHER: "I'm thinking that either I have done something terrible that you don't want to tell me about or that you need your friends so badly that you have to continue to act up just to look good to them. I'm wondering if you would be happier with a different teacher, or a different place to sit in the classroom, or what . . . What are your thoughts?"

(This is not a statement you would make if you have concerns about actually making a change in a classroom assignment.)

8. These techniques usually solve the problem.

In the event that they don't, consider reassigning one or more of these students. There are times in which the best solution is to break up the group. It never serves the best interest of the child, the class or the teacher for a group to stay together when it has become dysfunctional. This is a time when the teacher needs to set aside a personal feeling of "not wanting to give up" on a child or problem.

Even though this approach looks at eight different concepts, the most important aspect of this problem still goes back to the quality of the relationship between the teacher and the student. Students who have a strong level of caring for their teachers are usually willing to become more cooperative when invited to do so. A coercive or adversarial classroom climate tends to encourage negative group behavior when there are several students who lack confidence to be successful in the classroom.

The Use of the "Recovery Process" for Disruptive Classroom Students

The "Recovery Process" is one of the nine skills found in the multimedia training program, 9 Essential Skills for the Love and Logic Classroom®. An in-depth study of this technique can be found on pages 29-40 in the *9 Essential Skills for the Love and Logic Classroom*® workbook.

We have found that the Recovery Process loses its effectiveness when used with students who are not doing their assignments. The Recovery Process is not designed to punish, but is used strictly to eliminate annoying or disruptive behaviors.

Students who are uninvolved in their lessons but not bothering others, should remain in the classroom as long as their behavior is not interfering with the learning process. The fact that these students aren't doing their assignment doesn't mean that they're not soaking up at least some of the teacher's wisdom.

Unskilled teachers, or those who lack understanding of the brain's role in learning, often fear that a student's lack of involvement in the lesson will rub off on others, causing them to not want to learn. These teachers hold to the belief that kids don't want to learn in the first place and must be forced to do so. However, off-task behavior has far more to do with unfulfilled basic needs and personal problems than a desire not to learn. It is a rare kid who has a goal of becoming a failure.

In the event that another student in the classroom asks, "Why do I have to do the assignment? He isn't doing the work. Why can't I do the same thing?" the skilled teacher simply replies, "Maybe you can do the same thing. All you need to do is bring a note from your parents telling me that you don't need to learn anything in my classroom, and I will consider it."

Reminders:
• The Recovery Process is not designed to force kids to do their assignments.
• The Recovery Process is not designed to cure kids of emotional problems.

- The Recovery Process is strictly used to minimize a student's ability to interfere with learning and/or teaching.
- A student should not get personal attention from an adult while in Recovery. This time should be devoted to getting one's self back together. Students should get time with adults when doing what is right, not when misbehaving.
- Do not send work with the student to do during Recovery.
- The attitude of the teacher should be: "You are welcome to be with us for every good minute—this means every minute you are not making it difficult for me to teach or for others to learn. You are welcome to use "Recovery" to get yourself back together. We want you in the classroom, so return just as soon as you know that you can be here without bothering anyone else."

Effective use of the other essential skills of the Love and Logic classroom usually reduces the need to apply the Recovery Process. Building positive relationships with difficult kids is absolutely essential.

Kids who are willing to annoy the teacher are the ones who most desperately need to develop a positive relationship with that teacher. For this, you will want to implement the essential skill, "The One Sentence Intervention."

This skill can be found in *9 Essential Skills for the Love and Logic Classroom*®. It is also presented in the book *Teaching with Love and Logic*.

NOTE: It is wise to build the Recovery Process into the Functional Behavior Support Plan for special education students. Until such time, give this child the opportunity to take work with him/her if the child so desires. (Children usually don't beg to take work with them.)

It is not uncommon for kids who carry a heavy load of personal, family, and emotional problems to need several trips to a Recovery setting each day. This is an indication of a strong need for counseling or therapy. These kids are best reached by building a positive relationship with them, not in trying to overpower them.

The true test of whether or not the Recovery Process is working resides in answers to these questions: "Can the teacher teach while the student is in Recovery?" and "Can others learn without disruption while the student is in Recovery?" If the answer to both of these questions is yes, then the process is working. Don't expect the Recovery Process to cure the problems behind misbehavior or lack of motivation.

This attitude differentiates Recovery from "Time-Out." The Time-Out process allows the teacher to decide when the student can return. The Recovery Process allows the student to decide when to return. However, if the student returns with a bad attitude, he/she should be sent back to Recovery to do a better job of repairing his/her attitude.

When sending a student to Recovery, be sure to say, "You get back here just as soon as you can. We want you back with us." Consistently making this statement can eliminate a source of problems with parents who might accuse the teacher of denying their child an education by excluding him/her from the classroom.

Remedy for Tardy Students

What Does Not Work
The following have been used for years with little or no positive results:

- Punishment
- Lectures
- Warnings
- Sending kids to the office
- Rewards
- Detention
- Suspensions
- Keeping kids after school
- Taking kids and parents to court

For Best Results
- Build a positive teacher-pupil relationship so that the student would rather be with the teacher than elsewhere.
- The first five minutes of class time should be devoted to an exercise for which the student is held accountable. This exercise is one that cannot be made up at a later date. This is a good time for the kids to work with other students to complete an assignment made up of several review questions. This meets some needs of the child, as well as providing valuable reinforcement for learning.
- These assignments must be turned in for points toward the student's grade at a specific time. It is often helpful for students to correct each other's papers to eliminate additional work for the teacher.
- The teacher stands in front of the classroom door, greeting students, and providing the three elements of love:
  - Eye contact
  - Smiles
  - Touch in the form of handshakes, high fives, etc.

- The teacher greets students with:
  - "Good morning. Good to see you."
  - "Good morning. Glad you made it."
  - "Good to see you. We missed you yesterday."

In the Event the Student Is Tardy:

This is key to the success of this approach. The teacher moves toward the student, smiles, and says, "I'm glad you made it. I was worried about you."

- Do not reprimand.
- Do not punish.

This is the way to handle it, even if the student is extremely late. Sorrow can be expressed for his/her missing the opening assignment.

Remember that the student is never allowed to make up the opening assignment regardless of the value of the excuse. Say, "I'm sorry you missed it, but maybe you'll have a chance to earn some points tomorrow when you get here on time."

The problems associated with tardiness should rest squarely on the shoulder of the person who is tardy.

The responsibility of making the first five minutes of class time too valuable for a student to miss should rest squarely on the shoulder of the teacher.

Involving other staff members such as counselors, administrators, etc., is a waste of valuable time and money. I have rarely seen this to be effective in cases of tardiness.

Kids who continue to have problems with being late are probably indicating that something is going wrong in their lives and need to have the teacher spend some time working with them. This time should be spent in problem-solving rather than in a punitive way. **The ultimate solution will come through the relationship the teacher builds with the student, not through punitive measures.**

A school is not a prison.

---

9 Essential Skills for The Love and Logic Classroom®

Developed by Jim Fay and Charles Fay, Ph.D.

1. Neutralizing Student Arguing
2. Delayed Consequence
3. Empathy
4. The Recovery Process
5. Developing Positive Teacher-Student Relationships
6. Setting Limits with Enforceable Statements
7. Using Choices to Prevent Power Struggles
8. Quick and Easy Preventive Interventions
9. Guiding Students to Own and Solve Their Problems

Neutralizing Student Arguing
ESSENTIAL SKILL CATEGORY ONE: KEY FACTS

Goals of this skill category:

• Help educators understand that trying to reason or lecture with upset or resistant students is fruitless—and always makes things worse.

• Help students learn that manipulation is a poor way to get what they want.

• Give educators some specific phrases or "one-liners" they can use to teach students that they will not argue or give in.

• Provide educators with a foundation for effectively handling students' arguing about the other new Love and Logic skills they will be learning.

Jim and Charles emphasize that:

This skill must be learned first!

Sub-skills:
- Learn how to go "brain dead" and resist the urge to think about the manipulation.
- Memorize a Love and Logic "one-liner."
- Physically disengage from the student.

Common mistakes and misconceptions:
- This is not designed to help teachers "get even with" students.
- This is not designed to be done with sarcasm or anger.
- Use these skills only when kids are manipulating—not when they are hurting or are expressing disagreement in a respectful manner.

Delayed Consequences
ESSENTIAL SKILL CATEGORY TWO: KEY FACTS

Goals of this skill category:
- Give educators a response they can use when they don't know how to respond to something a student has done, or when they are too frustrated to think straight.
- Provide a skill that allows educators to gain suggestions and support from other adults before providing consequences.
- Debunk the myth that consequences must always come immediately.
- Encourage educators to avoid telling students exactly what consequences they will receive in advance.

Jim and Charles emphasize that:
When students are wondering what a consequence will be, they have far less energy to sabotage it.

Sub-skills:
- Embrace the belief that it's okay for a student to think he or she has gotten away with something.
- Create a classroom discipline plan that allows students to think harder about consequences than you do.

- When problems arise, students can pick solutions—not consequences.
- Develop between five and eight values that will guide your disciplinary decisions.
- Communicate your plan to parents in a letter similar to Mrs. Krochmal's.

Common mistakes and misconceptions:
- We must always say something to misbehaving students when they are acting up.
- It's always wrong to use immediate consequences.

Empathy
ESSENTIAL SKILL CATEGORY THREE: KEY FACTS

Goals of this skill category:
- Give educators a skill that will dramatically decrease student anger, resentment, revenge and passive-aggressive behavior.
- Help educators replace automatic anger reactions with automatic empathetic ones.
- Meet the universal human need for unconditional respect and love.
- Show educators a way to be powerful and caring at the very same time.
- Empathy, followed by silence, is a great way to get others thinking and talking.

Jim and Charles emphasize that:
Teachers who use the Love and Logic approach without empathy aren't using the Love and Logic approach!

Sub-skills:
- Memorize just one empathetic statement.
- Delay consequences when you are too angry or frustrated to be empathetic.
- Review this skill when you find yourself slipping into old habits.
- Resist pressure by other adults to "get tough" with students.
- Look forward to misbehavior—so that we can experiment with new skills.

Common mistakes and misconceptions:
- Providing empathy *after* rather than *before* consequences
- Using either sarcasm or sympathy
- Thinking that kids will suddenly become angels if we use this skill correctly
- Believing that it's never okay to put some steel into one's voice or to express anger in a healthy way

---

The Recovery Process
ESSENTIAL SKILL CATEGORY FOUR: KEY FACTS

Goals of this skill category:
- Give educators a process designed to preserve the learning environment when a student's, or students', behavior is making it impossible to teach.
- Help educators learn to implement it without being punitive.
- Encourage them to work together by adapting this process to their unique school.

Jim and Charles emphasize that:
The recovery process is not designed as a punishment or consequence that will modify the child's behavior, attitude, or motivation to complete work.

Sub-skills:
- Identify two or more colleagues who will help you implement this process.
- Meet and discuss the exercise "Plugging the Holes in Your Recovery Plan."
- Know how to respond when a student says, "I'm not leaving!" (Meet and discuss the workbook exercise "I'm Not Leaving! You Can't Make Me!".)
- Know how to send students by using empathy and whispering.

Common mistakes and misconceptions:
- Using Recovery as a first resort, before implementing other preventative measures

• Using threats, lectures or repeated warnings
• Talking to the student in ways that allow the rest of the class to hear what is being said
• Using it to get even with students
• Expecting it to cure students or to make them enthusiastic about learning

Some Special Reminders about Recovery from Jim Fay

The "Recovery Process" is not designed to make students do their assignments. It is also not designed to punish, but is used **strictly to eliminate annoying or disruptive behaviors.**

Students who are uninvolved in their lessons, but not bothering others should remain in the classroom as long as their behavior is not interfering with the learning process. The fact that these students aren't doing their assignments doesn't mean that they're not soaking up at least some of the teacher's wisdom.

Unskilled teachers, or those who lack understanding of the brain's role in learning, often fear that a student's lack of involvement in the lesson will rub off on others, causing them to not want to learn. These teachers hold to the belief that kids don't want to learn in the first place and must be forced to do so. However, off-task behavior has far more to do with unfulfilled basic needs and personal problems than a desire not to learn. It is a rare kid who has a goal of becoming a failure.

In the event that another student ever asks, "Why do I have to do the assignment? He isn't doing the work. Why can't I do the same thing?" the skilled teacher simply replies, "Maybe you can do the same thing. All you need to do is bring a note from your parents telling me that you don't need to learn anything in my classroom, and I will consider it."

Reminders:
• The Recovery Process is not designed to force kids to do their assignments.
• The Recovery Process is not designed to cure kids of emotional problems.
• The Recovery Process is strictly used to minimize a student's ability to interfere with learning and/or teaching.

- A student should not get personal attention from an adult while in Recovery. This time should be devoted to getting one's self back together. Students should get time with adults when doing what is right, not when misbehaving.
- Do not send work with the student to do during Recovery.
- The attitude of the teacher should be: "You are welcome to be with us for every good minute—this means every minute you are not making it difficult for me to teach or for others to learn. You are welcome to use "Recovery" to get yourself back together. We want you in the classroom, so return as soon as you know that you can be here without bothering anyone else."
- **Effective use of the other essential skills of the Love and Logic classroom usually reduces the need to apply the Recovery Process. Building positive relationships with difficult kids is absolutely essential.**
- **Kids who are willing to annoy the teacher are the ones who most desperately need to develop a positive relationship with that teacher. For this you will want to implement the essential skill, "The One Sentence Intervention."**
- **This skill can be found in** *9 Essential Skills for the Love and Logic Classroom*. **It is also presented in** *Teaching with Love and Logic.*
- It is wise to build the Recovery Process into the Functional Behavior Plan for special education students. Until such time, give this child the opportunity to take work with him/her if the child so desires. (They usually don't beg to take work with them.)
- It is not uncommon for kids who carry a heavy load of personal, family, and emotional problems to need several trips to a Recovery setting each day. This is an indication of a strong need for counseling or therapy. These kids are best reached by building a positive relationship with them, not in trying to overpower them.
- The true test of whether or not the Recovery Process is working resides in these questions: "Can the teacher teach while the student is in Recovery?" and, "Can others learn without disruption while the student is in Recovery?" If the answer to each of these questions is yes, then the process is working. **Don't expect the Recovery Process to cure the problems behind misbehavior or lack of motivation.**

- This attitude differentiates Recovery from Time-Out. The Time-Out Process allows the teacher to decide when the student can return. The Recovery Process allows the student to decide when to return. However, if the student returns with a bad attitude, he/she should be sent back to Recovery to do a better job of repairing his/her attitude.
- When sending a student to Recovery, be sure to say, "You get back here just as soon as you can. We want you back with us." Consistently making this statement can eliminate a source of problems with parents who might accuse the teacher of denying their child an education by excluding them from the classroom.

Positive Teacher-Student Relationships
ESSENTIAL SKILL CATEGORY FIVE: KEY FACTS

Goals of this skill category:
- Help educators see why positive relationships form the foundation of effective classroom management and academic achievement motivation.
- Give them specific skills for developing these relationships.
- Provide alternatives to using praise, which tends to backfire with tough students.
- Help educators understand why some kids act worse when we begin this skill.

Jim and Charles emphasize that:
Teachers who use relationships to manipulate students into being good quickly find that students are too smart for this. Relationships are meant to be sincere and reciprocal.

Sub-skills:
- Greet students at the door each day and use the three elements of human bonding.
- Apply the "One Sentence Intervention."
- Keep trying even when students get worse or don't reciprocate.

Common mistakes and misconceptions:
• Trying to build relationships by noticing only good behavior and achievement
• Expecting tough kids to reciprocate immediately
• Expecting that students will immediately improve academically
• Trying to be a friend rather than a caring authority figure
• Believing that this will change the student's "self-concept"

Setting Limits with Enforceable Statements
ESSENTIAL SKILL CATEGORY SIX: KEY FACTS

Goals of this skill category:
• Help educators understand that they risk giving away their power when they issue orders or rules they cannot enforce.
• Give them specific statements that increase student thinking rather than resistance.
• Train students to listen to their teachers—rather than ignore them.
• Show educators how to enforce limits with questions.

Jim and Charles emphasize that:
Limits are enforced most effectively through works rather than words.

Sub-skills:
• Create some of your own enforceable statements using the exercise, "Setting Limits with Enforceable Statements."
• Expect that some students will argue, even when you use these statements.
• Be prepared to neutralize arguing by applying the skills discussed in module one.
• Don't go overboard. Set only those limits you absolutely need—and can enforce.

Common mistakes and misconceptions:

• Believing that enforceable statements will make students behave
• Applying them with a sarcastic, angry or dictatorial attitude
• Giving repeated reminders or warnings
• Trying to use too many enforceable statements rather than experimenting with just a handful

---

Using Choices to Prevent Power Struggles
ESSENTIAL SKILL CATEGORY SEVEN: KEY FACTS

Goals of this skill category:

• Help educators understand that control is such a strong emotional need that students will get it met regardless of what it takes.
• Provide educators with specific strategies for helping students meet this need in a healthy way.
• Give educators practical guidelines for presenting effective choices within limits.
• Give students plenty of opportunities to think and make affordable mistakes.

Jim and Charles emphasize that:

The most important rule for giving choices is to provide the vast majority of them when it's convenient for you and the students are behaving well.

Sub-skills:

• Identify common power struggles that occur in your classroom.
• As a preventative measure, develop an appropriate choice for each.
• Experiment by providing this choice before the students become resistant.

Common mistakes and misconceptions

• Believing that giving choices is wimpy or permissive
• Ignoring the fact that choices are given only *with limits*

- Giving choices after resistance rather than before it
- Expecting that giving choices will always cause students to make good choices

---

Quick and Easy Preventative Interventions
ESSENTIAL SKILL CATEGORY EIGHT: KEY FACTS

Goals of this skill category:
- Help educators understand that success comes from preventing behavior problems rather than reacting to them.
- Provide educators with specific strategies for preventing disruptions without stopping the flow of instruction.
- Give educators guidelines for when to apply these interventions.
- Help teachers avoid unnecessary, time-consuming confrontations with students.

Jim and Charles emphasize that:
Preventative interventions gain their full power when teachers have also invested in building positive relationships.

Sub-skills:
- Structure the physical layout of the classroom so that you can easily circulate among your students.
- Constantly scan the classroom to obtain as much visual contact with students as possible.
- Resist the urge to ignore minor instances of misbehavior.

Common mistakes and misconceptions:
- Believing that ignoring misbehavior actually works
- Allowing misbehavior to escalate or spread before intervening
- Trying to use all of the preventative interventions each time a student misbehaves
- Teaching from a place in the room that limits teacher movement

Guiding Students to Own and Solve Their Problems
ESSENTIAL SKILL CATEGORY NINE: KEY FACTS

Goals of this skill category:
- Help educators understand the difference between the Helicopter, Drill Sergeant, and Consultant styles.
- Give educators a five-step process for guiding students to solve their problems.
- Encourage educators to develop problem-solving suggestions for their most common student problems before students come to them with these problems.
- Provide guidelines for when it's appropriate to use this skill.
- Teach students that they're capable of being in control of their lives.

Jim and Charles emphasize that:
Students are always better prepared for life when they are required to think harder about their problems than we do.

Sub-skills:
- Be prepared with a variety of suggestions for solving common student problems by completing the exercise, "Some Students Decide To . . . "
- Provide a lousy solution first so that students experience control by rejecting it.
- Remember that you don't need to complete all five steps in the same sitting.
- It's okay to take some time and ask other professionals to help you develop a menu of suggestions to provide the student.

Common mistakes and misconceptions:
- Thinking that we must use this entire process every time a student has a problem
- Expecting that this process will force students to solve their problems well
- Telling students which solutions they should use

QUASI MANDATING PARENT TRAINING

Parent Training for Kindergarten Parents

Several years I got a call from David Kaufman, principal of a Love and Logic School in Raytown, Missouri.

"Jim I've got to tell you what I did three years ago. I got the Love and Logic parent training curriculum and I mandated that parents of Kindergarten students take a parenting course."

"Oh, David, you can't mandate something like that."

"Yeah, I know. That's what my secretary told me. So I told her that it was only a quasi mandate. I just told her to act like taking a Love and Logic parenting course was what all of the parents of kindergarten kids did at this school.

"She made two sign-up sheets. One sign was for kindergarten enrollment, and the other was for parent class enrollment. When parents came in to enroll their kids for school, she'd say, 'by the way, parents of kindergarten kids at this school take this parenting course. Which one do you want, the evening class or the day-time class?'

"She reported that most of the parents answered by saying, 'Oh, okay. That's good.'

"The parents enjoyed the class and told their friends that they ought to try to get in it."

"But David, what did she say to parents who didn't want to sign up?"

"Oh she just told them that we'd miss them, and that they could take the course some other time if they were interested, but she didn't have to do that very often."

"Wow, David. How did it work out?"

"You know, Jim, I think it's one of the better things we've done. After three years, I can truthfully say that the parents who've taken the course are much more supportive of the school and far less critical. It really helps for them to have a better understanding of what we do and why we do it."

Since those days, David and I have shared this technique with thousands of schools. Principals who have used this approach say the same thing, that parents who take the course are more supportive and less critical of their schools. And who doesn't need that?

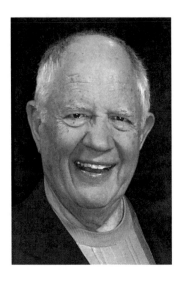

Jim Fay

The legendary Jim Fay began his career as a teacher, and for over three decades served in public, private, and parochial schools. He spent seventeen years as a school principal and administrator, and for nearly thirty years has served as an educational consultant and public speaker.

Jim's teaching experience in both inner city and suburban schools revealed a need to structure the educational environment in a way that would build positive relationships with students. This structure also had to address the need to teach children responsibility and self-discipline, and at the same time keep educators from being labeled as "mean." To meet this need, Jim devised the Love and Logic technique for use in both homes and classrooms.

One of Jim's goals is to give educators the skills they need to return home at the end of the day with energy left over for themselves and their families. Because of his experience and ability to help educators, Jim has won many awards in the education field.

Index